UNTIGERING

Peaceful Parenting for the Deconstructing Tiger Parent

by Iris Chen

For more information about this author, please visit www.untigering.com

Cover design: Julia Kestner
Interior design: Priya Paulraj

Editor: Olga Knezivic

ISBN: 9798571817721

To my parents,
my partner Jason,
and my children Noah and Caleb—
three generations who are untigering together.

CONTENTS

FOREWORD

I ris and I are both Asian, both mothers, and our husbands even share the same name and almost the same birthday. But that's where the similarities end. She's introverted, I'm extroverted. I am fast, loud, and clamor for attention, while she's steady, grounded, and invites participation. Yet we somehow ended up as kindred spirits, each writing about our unique experiences and challenges within the gentle parenting space.

I began my writing career in the early 2010s as some popular authors emerged from the faith blogging scene. As I practiced my craft of writing, I imitated the voices of other bloggers, a common path for many writers as we write our way to our own voice. The glaring problem, which was immediately noticeable to me, was that the prominent voices were all white.

When I shifted into writing about parenting, the problem was even worse. Parenting literature is even more white-dominant than stories about faith. I worked hard to decolonize my own voice, navigating the intricate calculations many people of color are familiar with: how much to cater to the white audience with buying power; how much to insert my own stories knowing it will sound foreign and perhaps not resonate as well; how to be myself without making white people uncomfortable.

Along comes Iris Chen, with her unapologetically Asian tagline: UNTIGERING. "I hope my white readers will find universal resonance as I write out of my particular experience," she tells me. And I wish I had that kind of casual audacity to speak bravely as a person with multiple intersectional identities.

Gentle parenting, peaceful parenting, and its many iterations of similar branding have public white-representing faces, and that in itself is a parenting problem. If parents are consuming predominantly white voices to guide their parenting, our kids are internalizing whiteness as the norm, and we fail to break the cycle of systemic racism.

Untigering isn't just a book about anti-racism, it's a guide to raising children with justice from Iris's perspective, a voice we need to include on our parenting literature shelves. The best parenting practice isn't done in the direction *of* our children but is a journey inwards, towards our own path of healing and growth. Attempting to change our children will end in frustration, but we can change ourselves for a better path forward. Some authors are gurus, giving us "aha" moments and inspiring us towards deep reflection. Others are professors, teaching us how to do the work. Iris manages to combine both of these roles as she walks us through both the why-you-need-to-do-this-work and the here's-how-to-do-it. She gives us containers, the vocabulary to name our unique family stories; and because of these containers, she gives us the capacity to create new stories that are more closely aligned with the values we want for ourselves and for our children.

Untigering seeks to treat our children better by doing the deep examination of our own parental instincts and patterns. None of us will be able to finish this work-of-a-lifetime, but we won't be able to begin unless we can describe what we're doing. Iris prompts us to "write a brave new ending" to our stories, some of which have been marked by trauma, oppression, and injustice. The magical part about our courage to write better endings is that it breathes life into our children. Popular parenting sentiments often quip that every generation deals with different challenges and struggles; we joke that the best parenting hack is to save up for therapy for our kids. The implication is that it's not actually possible to do better, that we're simply exchanging one set of struggles for another. I find this to be fatalistic and untrue. While it's true that the work of justice for children is long and likely will take more than one generation, the work that we do in our lifetime matters to us, our children, and their children. We are pushing forward a tide of progress in the way we view and treat children.

The thing about the work of both parenting and justice is that they are both marathons in which it's sometimes difficult to discern short-term gains. It's a lot harder, in the short term, to parent a willful child expressing the full range of her emotions than it is to manage a child whose spirit has been broken enough to obey and do as he's told. So those of us who are committed to this work have to give each other regular reminders: it's worth it, it matters, it will make a world of difference.

What you're about to read in the following pages is worth it, it matters, it will make a world of difference. I'm so grateful that the children you encounter are going to be treated with more compassion and love because of it.

Cindy Wang Brandt
author of *Parenting Forward: How to Raise Children with Justice, Mercy, and Kindness*

PREFACE

Hi! I'm Iris.

Here are a few things you should know about me and this book:

I am an American Born Chinese who ended up with Chinese Born American kids.

My parents were immigrants from Hong Kong and Vietnam who came to America in search of opportunities. I was the first of their children to be born in the States and was well on my way to fulfilling the "American Dream"—graduating from a top-notch university and marrying a Silicon Valley engineer—when my partner and I did an about-face and headed out to China to teach English to college students. We went in 2003, thinking we'd give it a year. We ended up staying for sixteen. China is where my kids were born and where they grew up; it is the context in which I was baptized into adulthood and motherhood.

This book is about me learning to navigate life and parenting at the intersection of my Chinese and American identities. Throughout the book, I talk about being a child of immigrants, share my experiences of growing up as a Chinese American, relate stories of living in China, discuss Chinese culture, and use the Chinese language. While this book is for anyone who is trying to divest from tiger parenting, it was really important for me to center my own perspective as a person of color (POC), especially as there are so few parenting books out there that are written through this lens. My hope is that Asian American and other POC parents will feel seen and represented through my story. For those who might think this book is not for you, I challenge you to stretch your imagination, expand your understanding, and open yourself to other perspectives.

I am a deconstructing tiger mother who is trying to become a peaceful parent.

My early years of motherhood were fraught with authoritarian, abusive practices. Yelling, spanking, punishing with unreasonable consequences—anything was game as long as I showed my kids who was boss. But far from my dreams of raising a well-behaved, obedient child, my eldest son fought back at every turn, resisting my attempts to control and manipulate him. The behavioral issues only intensified when I became stricter and punished harder, but that was all I knew to do.

When I finally recognized the trauma that I was causing my child through my harsh parenting, I was forced to confront the bitter truth: the problem was not with my son, but with me. If I had any hope of healing my relationship with him, I was the one who had to change.

So I did another about-face and dove into learning more about gentle, peaceful parenting. I stopped using violence, punishments, and even rewards. I became an advocate for treating children with dignity, respect, and compassion.

This book is about my awkward, clumsy steps toward peaceful parenting. I wrote it for other deconstructing tiger parents like me—"untigering" dads and moms and caretakers who are trying to break free from authoritarian family dynamics and cultural norms; parents and adults who are learning to honor children and fight against their oppression. I am on that same journey.

Unlike many parenting books written by authors with degrees and titles attached to their names, I'm simply a fellow parent on a similar journey. I have no expert opinion or professional advice; just reflections on my own untigering process and lessons that I've learned along the way. But I am encouraged by the fact that we don't have to be researchers or academics to do this work of untigering. We can access our own intuition and inner wisdom, listen to our children, and learn from the cycle-breakers who have gone before us.

I am a recovering overachiever who is unschooling with her kids.

I was a precocious child who read at an early age, skipped kindergarten, became my high school valedictorian, attended a prestigious university, and graduated with honors... a semester early. I fully expected my children to follow in my footsteps.

Fortunately, my journey into peaceful parenting challenged me to rethink my hopes and dreams for my children. As I learned to honor my children's individuality and autonomy, it no longer made sense to subject them to a system that wouldn't do the same. As I began to trust in their innate ability and motivation to learn, I no longer believed in a compulsory education that forced children to comply to arbitrary adult standards.

I made yet another U-turn, rejecting all the clambering for success and achievement that I had grown up with. I took my kids out of formal schooling and started giving them space to self-direct their learning and their lives. What began as an experiment has become an unschooling lifestyle and a personal passion.

Akilah S. Richards, podcaster and speaker, defines unschooling as a "child-trusting, anti-oppression, liberatory, love-centered approach to parenting and caregiving."[1] This book is written through this anti-op-

pression and social justice lens and thus goes beyond simply redefining success and education. It seeks to honor a child's autonomy in every area of their lives. It recognizes the unequal power and dominance that characterizes the way we often engage with children and challenges that "adultism"—exposing the ways we oppress children and then justify our domination over them. My hope is that this book will help us change our view of children and teach us to see them as human beings worthy of the same respect we ourselves expect to receive.

What this book is NOT

This is not a "how-to" book about how to get your kids to behave or change. There are no simple formulas, easy steps, standard scripts, or quick fixes. If you're looking for 5 easy ways to get your child to eat broccoli or sleep through the night, you will be sorely disappointed!

Rather, we will question together why we dehumanize, manipulate, and disrespect children, even for their "own good." We will do the hard work of challenging our assumptions, seeing with new eyes, healing our wounds, and transforming ourselves.

Take my hand. Let's begin untigering together.

INTRODUCTION

"**N**oah, it's time for your nap. Lie down. Face the wall."

"But Mama, I can't sleep. I'm not tired."

My toddler does not understand that his nap time has little to do with how tired he is and a lot to do with how tired Mama is. All I ever think about is the amount of sleep I'm (not) getting. I will not be thwarted from securing my few precious moments of child-free quiet time.

Time to double down.

"You need your nap... Or do I need to take out The Spatula?" The Spatula is the free plastic rice paddle that we had received as a bonus gift with our purchase of packaged ramen. You can probably guess how we had repurposed it.

"Mama..."

"No talking. Go to sleep. Say, '*Yes, Mama.*'"

"Yes, Mama," he mimics.

But his verbal assent does not translate into immediate action. When he turns toward me, I flip him back to face the wall. When he squirms too much, I give him a swift swat. After what seems like hours, he finally drifts off and I slowly slink off the bed, careful not to wake him.

My relief is premature.

I make it halfway to the door before he pops up, wide awake. I feel like a criminal on house arrest, any endeavor to leave the premises setting off alarms in my son's body.

"Go back to sleep!"

I attempt to make a hasty retreat, but he attaches himself to my leg like an ankle bracelet. Peeling him off and depositing him on top of the changing table, I slam the door and hold it closed, determined to not let him out even if he does manage to climb down.

He starts wailing.

"Calm down! Stop screaming!" The irony doesn't occur to me as I scream at him through the door, decidedly not calm.

I look at my watch. It's only 10 o'clock in the morning.

I never meant to be a tiger mother. But as a young Chinese American mother living in China, the odds were against me. After all, it was in my blood... and in the water.

I had grown up in Canada and the States, a child of Chinese immigrant parents from Hong Kong and Vietnam. By white parenting standards, my mother and father would have been considered oppressive dictators: I wasn't allowed to watch TV without permission, talk back to my father without dire consequences, or have a boyfriend before college. In high school, my friends even created the ILO (Iris Liberation Organization) to try to sneak me out of my house on weeknights. They failed.

By Chinese standards, however, my parents' strictness was what made them good parents... or at least effective ones. I performed well at school, never hung out with the "wrong crowd," played the piano, graduated from a renowned university, and married another Chinese American who also ticked all the boxes. In the eyes of many, my parents had succeeded.

"Chinese parenting" was all I had ever known, save for the glimpses of Western family dynamics that I had seen on *Growing Pains*, in Beverly Cleary books, or during those awkward visits to my white friends' homes where their parents wanted me to call them by their first names. So, when I became a mother myself, my over-achieving tiger-mom instincts kicked in. It looked different than my parents'—I did plan on adding some Western elements, like saying the occasional "I love you" or allowing them to go to their senior prom—but the spirit was essentially the same:

Mama knows best. Say, "Yes, Mama."

I expected obedience and compliance and used whatever means necessary to achieve it. I bribed, I lectured, I spanked, I sent them to their rooms, I withheld privileges—all in the name of discipline. Noah, in particular, refused to fall in line, but I refused to back down. Our home became a battleground of endless power struggles, uncontrollable tantrums, and constant frustration. There was so much conflict and stress that I was losing the ability to enjoy my children.

Motherhood was ruining my straight-A reputation.

What is Untigering?

The term "tiger mother" comes from Amy Chua's controversial 2011 memoir, *Battle Hymn of the Tiger Mother*.[2] Chua, a Yale law professor, sparked an international debate about parenting when she wrote about her exploits in strict "Chinese parenting," pitting it against the stereotypically indulgent parenting style of the West. The practice of tiger parenting, however, dates back much further and extends beyond those of Chinese descent. It is parenting that is utilitarian and authoritarian. Strategies like psychological, behavioral, and physical control are exerted over the child. Extremely high expectations for a child's behavior and performance are the norm, particularly in the area of academics. Emotional warmth and empathy are lacking, but punishment, shame, or withdrawal of affection are ready tools.

I raised my kids for many years in China, the land of tiger mothers. There, it's just called *parenting*.[3] Driven by the culture around me, my family background, authoritarian religion, and my own personality, I bought into tiger parenting and the cultivation of obedience by whatever means necessary. But despite all my efforts to get things right, things were going horribly wrong. My relationship with Noah was deteriorating by the day.

Then one day, a psychologist friend of mine came into town to give a parenting seminar for local Chinese families. I went to show her support, not realizing that it would end up being a turning point in my own parenting. She showed us pictures of brain scans and explained how the limbic system in a child's brain lights up when they're upset and emotionally dysregulated. She told us that when we as parents then react with anger, yelling, violence, threats, or punishment, we trigger their fear response and further stimulate their "emotional brain," making it even more difficult for them to calm down and rationalize.

My mind was blown. This was the first time anyone had connected biology and brain development to parenting for me. My eyes were opened to how the problem was actually with me and not with my child. His reactions were completely normal, but the ways I was reacting to my child's meltdowns were exacerbating and escalating the storm inside his brain and body. I had been punishing him when what he really needed was my help. All that time, I had assumed Noah had been *giving* me a hard time instead of recognizing that he was *having* a hard time.

Armed with this newfound knowledge, I knew that I was at a crossroads. I could dig in my heels and continue down the path I was on (the very definition of insanity), or I could defect from the tiger mom camp and find a better way. I chose the latter. That very night, I went home and told my partner, Jason, I was going to stop spanking.

That was the beginning of my untigering journey.

Untigering Definition

I think of untigering as a two-fold practice of:

1. detoxing from being tiger-parented and
2. detoxing from being a tiger parent.

It is the process of unlearning and dismantling tiger parenting so that we can practice peaceful parenting. It requires us to look back and address our childhood wounds, consider the present and what cycles need to be broken, and look ahead for how we hope to change the narrative for our children. It calls for us to question societal and cultural norms that are rooted in trauma and oppression so that generations after us can walk in greater freedom.

Let's flesh this out a bit more in the context of other parenting styles. In the field of (Western) psychology, parenting styles are typically divided into 4 categories.[4]

Authoritarian Parenting: "No-Give"

Such parents are strict, demanding, inflexible, and unresponsive to their child—the archetypal tiger parent. Their goal is compliance, and they rely heavily on power, control, and punishment to achieve it. Children are expected to obey without hesitation, negotiation, or dissent. There is often an emphasis on achievements, performance, or anything that confers bragging rights—trophies, awards, scholarships, salaries, and careers of the doctor-lawyer-engineer-CEO variety.

This style is common in cultures where hierarchical social and political dynamics are the accepted norm. A society built on patriarchy, colonialism, or despotism will naturally beget a similar family structure. For many untigering parents, this parenting style is still the one we default to most readily and the one we have to strive the hardest to resist.

Permissive Parenting: "Give In"

Those with this parenting style are often warm and nurturing, but indulgent toward their child. They are reluctant to give guidance, set limits, and enforce boundaries. Their child's discomfort makes them uncomfortable. Their child's resistance makes them unsure.

Some of us who have been tiger parented adopt this style in reaction to our stifling upbringing. We want to give our children everything that we were deprived of when we were younger. Or, after recognizing the fallout from our authoritarian ways, we swing in the opposite direction.

Such parenting may teach us to be more gentle and respectful towards our children, but fails to equip our children with the tools to be gentle and respectful towards others. It often leads to entitled kids and parents who self-sacrifice in unhealthy ways.

Uninvolved Parenting: "Give Up"

Uninvolved parents have checked out. Perhaps childhood trauma has made it difficult to bond with their own children. Perhaps they feel inadequate to face the challenges of parenting. Whatever the reason, such parents are disconnected, unengaged, and unresponsive.

While the "Chinese mother" is seen as the classic tiger mom, the trope of the stoic and aloof "Chinese father" is an apt portrayal of an uninvolved parent. Gone for long hours at work (or perhaps even gone for long months back in Asia while leaving his parachute kids[5] in the States), he has washed his hands clean of the day-to-day affairs of raising his children.

Authoritative Parenting: "Give Some Ground"

This is traditionally believed to be the style of parenting that has the best outcomes. High expectations are married with high emotional responsiveness for a rational and balanced approach. Most of us are probably aiming for this happy medium. We want well-behaved and responsible children, but we also want emotional closeness with them.

Yet when I look at the description of an authoritative parent by Diana Baumrind, the clinical psychologist known for formulating these parenting prototypes, there is little that I resonate with:

> The authoritative parent attempts to direct the child's activities but in a rational, issue-oriented manner. She [the parent] encourages verbal give and take, shares with the child the reasoning behind her policy, and solicits his objections when he refuses to conform. Both autonomous self-will and disciplined conformity are valued. Therefore she exerts firm control at points of parent-child divergence, but does not hem the child in with restrictions. She enforces her own perspective as an adult, but recognizes the child's individual interests and special ways. The authoritative parent affirms the child's present qualities, but also sets standards for future conduct. She uses reason, power, and shaping by regime and reinforcement to achieve her objectives, and does not base her decisions on group consensus or the individual child's desires.[6]

Honestly, this parenting paradigm just sounds like tiger-parenting-lite. It still places all the power and authority in the hands of the adult. The parent "direct[s] the child's activities," "exerts firm control," "enforces *her* own perspective," and "uses reason, power, and shaping by regime and reinforcement to achieve *her* objectives" [emphasis added]. Any attempts to honor the child's self-will and autonomy appear to be mere lip service. Any ground given in allowing the child to express their objections and self-will still positions the parents firmly at the top of the hierarchy. Even the word "authoritative" assumes a posture of dominance and a power-over dynamic that ignores the agency of a child.

Thankfully, over 50 years have passed since Baumrind published her research, and hopefully we've made some strides in our understanding of human psychology, attachment, and parenting (including gender neutral pronouns when talking about parents!). I believe we need a much more radical reframing of our role as parents—one that does not rely on power to control, but on connection to influence. I'd like to suggest a fifth parenting style that represents the vision of what I'm working towards as an untigering parent.

Peaceful Parenting: "Give-and-Take"

"Give-and-take" is defined as (1) a free exchange of ideas or opinions and (2) the willingness to accept some of another person's ideas and give up some of your own.[7]

You can't have a free exchange of ideas unless you value everyone's voice. You won't be willing to compromise if you don't believe the other person's thoughts are valid. Give-and-take frames the parent-child relationship as one based on partnership rather than power dynamics. There is mutuality instead of monocracy, collaboration instead of control.

Instead of trying to conform a child (however nicely) to their standards, values, and objectives, parents who practice this style resist imposing their will onto their children, choosing instead to honor their child's autonomy. Children are not addressed simply in a "rational, issue-oriented manner," but with emotional attunement and understanding. Parents see themselves as empowering coaches rather than teachers with all the answers, facilitators rather than leaders with an agenda. Boundaries and limits are respected out of loving relationship, not because of arbitrary rules.

This kind of give-and-take is not a mathematical equation where we try to balance both sides equally. I am not talking about the kind of mutuality where the same expectations are placed upon children and adults alike without regard for development, experience, ability, or privilege. Peaceful parenting aims for equity, not equality.

Equality means everyone is treated the same, but equity means that everyone is given the support and empowerment they need to thrive. Babies are treated with special thought, attention, and tenderness. Teens are given extra compassion as they wrestle with their identities, their changing bodies, and their growing freedom. Parents who carry the mental load of the household are encouraged to take time to care for their personal needs. Those who have more power, privilege, and life experience (the adults) take on more responsibility and provide guidance. The family functions like a body with many parts, each part treated differently yet appropriately so that the whole body can flourish.

This style of parenting means that:

- **We look for win-win solutions instead of ones that only benefit one party.**
  As much as possible, we consider everybody's needs and engage our children in looking for solutions. We aren't just concerned with our own convenience or with enforcing our perspective, but see ourselves as part of a team.
- **We respect our child's boundaries as well as our own.**
  We know that we cannot control another person, so our focus is on controlling ourselves and the environment. We are clear about communicating our own boundaries as well as honoring our child's in ways that are safe and responsible.
- **We are willing to negotiate, compromise, and be flexible.**
  We don't rely on rigid rules but seek to respond appropriately based on the situation. Decisions are made based on the needs and desires of family members and are always up for discussion and adjustment.

- **We value the thoughts, opinions, and feelings of each individual, not just of those who hold the most power in the family.**
  It's never "my way or the highway." Each member is valuable, cared for, and empowered. Parents do not run roughshod over their children, but neither do children rule the roost.
- **We love and care for each other as we look out for each other's best interests.**
  It's ultimately about relationship and connection, not rules. There are times when we will need to mutually submit to one another out of care for one another. New parents may have to forgo their late-night parties so their baby can sleep. Children may have to take their craft outside so glitter doesn't get everywhere while Dad is making dinner. Such compromises are usually done willingly when motivated by love and not shoulds or musts.

This kind of parenting is very radical, even among parenting "experts." I find that a lot of parenting advice still focuses on manipulating children to get what you want, just in a nicer way. I'm not really interested in that. I believe we need to challenge the power dynamics within our family relationships that place parents over children. Just as with all social justice issues, those with more power need to be engaged in the work of giving away and sharing power.

Where does untigering fit?

It's easy to pit untigering against tiger parenting as if they were polar opposites, or equate untigering with peaceful parenting. In reality, untigering is neither. It's not a fixed parenting style, per se, but the process of transforming our parenting. It's the messy middle—the arduous journey rather than the destination, the process rather than the fixed state. It's the intention that we set every single day.

TIGER PARENTING		PEACEFUL PARENTING
Expects perfection		Embraces process
Enforces rules		Encourages relationship
Driven by success		Inspired by self-determination
Rigid		Flexible
Critical	UNTINGERING	Accepting
Controlling		Empowering
Harsh		Gentle, yet firm
Focuses on behavior		Focuses on needs
Demands		Models
Perpetuates oppression		Actively resists oppression

The arrow represents continual movement, growth, and transformation. The reason I chose the continuous verb form of *untigering* was to show this very idea. Despite the pressure to do things perfectly, the goal is not to "arrive." Rather, it's to—moment by moment, day by day—leave behind the dehumanizing, disconnecting, and coercive ways of tiger parenting while moving towards treating our children with love, respect, gentleness, kindness, and honor.

There's no need to feel shame or frustration at an impossible ideal. We *will* fail. We won't always live up to our principles. But we can continue to grow and move in the direction of our vision. There is no other choice for those of us who seek to parent without oppression. We must do the work.

Let's get started.

PART 1
CHANGING OUR STRIPES

CHAPTER 1

RECOGNIZING OUR STRIPES

We've all heard the saying, "A tiger cannot change its stripes." It's often used to disparage someone who's betrayed our trust—a cheating boyfriend, a dishonest business partner, a backstabbing friend. We've been betrayed one too many times and think that there's little hope for that person to change. Their predatory stripes can't be washed off.

Perhaps we have a similar view of ourselves. We don't believe we can change. We can't hold back our involuntary impulse to frown, cross our arms, or sigh disappointedly at our children. We can't stop ourselves from automatically answering "No!" to any request they have. We are tiger parents by nature and that's who we'll be forever and ever, amen.

Well, I'm here to tell you that we tiger parents *can* change our stripes.

But in order to do so, we have to change the limiting beliefs we have about ourselves.

Our Stripes Are Our Wounds

Our stripes are the patterns we've used to cope with our traumas. Just like a tiger's stripes, they are our way of surviving in an unfriendly environment, our way of masking ourselves to get our needs met and blending in to protect ourselves.

For POC who grew up in a white-dominated culture, we received many of our stripes simply by being "othered." When whiteness is considered the benchmark of beauty, strength, leadership, and charisma, those of us who don't conform are often overlooked or derided. We learn to assimilate in order to be accepted. We hide or alter our names, our food, our language, our culture, our family customs, and our physical features in an attempt to fit in. When our parents struggle to communicate in their limited English, shame. When we can't achieve that svelte Nordic physique with our stocky Cantonese genes, shame. Every day, in a hundred different ways, we receive messages telling us of how we fall short.

Other stripes we received simply by being human in a messy world. We may have had traumatic Adverse Childhood Experiences (ACEs)[8] like witnessing domestic violence or growing up with a mentally ill caregiver. Others of us experienced trauma that was less acute and dramatic but perhaps felt like "death by a thousand cuts." Even those of us who came from seemingly safe and stable homes may have suffered from having parents who were emotionally distant, verbally abusive, or uber-controlling.

For me, I learned early on as a child that relationships and emotions weren't safe. I saw the demeaning way the men in my family treated the women and it warped my view of marriage and intimacy. While I felt powerless to challenge my patriarchal elders, I began to distrust men and avoid emotional closeness. I vowed never to become the type of woman who would allow men to walk all over her. I promised never to love that type of man. The easiest way to do that was to keep people at arm's length—to be indifferent, to not get attached.

Multiple moves and uprootings by the age of 12 confirmed my belief that opening my heart up was too painful; it wasn't worth the risk. I opted to build a wall instead. Over the years, many friends considered me their BFF but I could never seem to reciprocate. Others moved on or grew apart from me, but I never grieved or shed a tear. My heart had begun to atrophy, like an underused muscle.

What had developed as a way to deal with pain I soon wore as a badge of honor. Relationships were for the weak. Dating was immature. I didn't need anyone—especially a boyfriend—to define my self-worth. No, I was an independent and self-sufficient woman. I rolled my eyes at those who dreamed of marriage and motherhood. I even considered celibacy for a season, so committed was I to this idea of being unattached. When I finally did get my first (and last) boyfriend at the ripe old age of 20, I broke the news to my friends with much embarrassment and shame. I wasn't as strong as I had thought.

My lack of healthy attachment continued into parenting. I loved my kids, but I had a hard time emotionally connecting to them. I knew how to feed them homemade baby food, sleep train them so they got 12 hours of nighttime sleep, and teach them how to read when they turned 4 years old—stuff that I felt I could measure and control and achieve. What I had never been taught was how to attune, empathize, and lovingly respond to my kids. They were just so needy, and I resented them for it. My childhood scars were not only hurting me, they were hurting my children.

So many of our stripes are actually the scars left behind by our wounds. They aren't an inherent part of us; they are trauma responses. Instead of recognizing that deep down, they do not reflect our truest selves, we learn to define ourselves through them, taking on what are essentially coping mechanisms as parts of our identity and "personality."

In order to change our stripes, we need to change our mind about ourselves. We are not held captive by our labels or destined to pass on toxic patterns. Our stripes may have helped us to survive but they are keeping us from thriving. Like in the KonMari method[9] where we sort our belongings, keeping only what "sparks joy" and thanking the items we throw away, we can thank these old patterns for how they have served us in the past and then toss them out to make space for what truly helps us flourish.

What are some of your stripes—ways that you've learned to define yourself? What resonates with who you are now, and what do you need to throw out? Find some time to reflect and write down your thoughts and observations.

Our Stripes Are Our Achievements

Our stripes also represent the ways we've defined ourselves by our achievements. We've earned our stripes through hard work and perseverance. Like the insignias on a military uniform, they immediately inform others where we rank and how successful we are.

Within our homes and families, we are often objectified and judged based on performance. I knew an auntie who would always introduce people by where they graduated from or what job they had. "Samuel here went to Northwestern!" "Katherine works at PWC." I found it awkward and reductionist, but not surprising. It's the tiger parenting way to identify people by their accomplishments. Outside our homes, the messages are the same. Patriarchy, capitalism, white supremacy, and systemic oppression further commodify us and enslave us to systems that require us to prove our worth over and over again.

All these stripes cause us to feel deeply insecure. We become afraid of failure and averse to risk. If we only receive attention and affection when we perform well, what happens when we don't? We'd rather not find out, so we keep up our manic pace of striving for success. We throw ourselves into pursuing advanced degrees, well-respected careers, prestigious accolades, and even super-mom status, not for any true enjoyment or expression of our intrinsic desires, but in order to gain approval. Our drive to outdo, outperform, and overachieve often has little to do with self-confidence and much to do with fear. Sadly, after we've burned or sold ourselves out, we pass on those same compulsions to our children.

We have lost our true selves when we go around collecting more and more stripes in order to prove that we are worthy of love. Untigering requires us to resist this urge to compete, compare, and classify. Even though most of us grew up in an environment where love was conditional, we have to unlearn the lie that our worth is tied to performance. The number on the report card, SAT exam, bathroom scale, or monthly paycheck is not a measure of our true value.

Our Stripes Are the Lies We Believe

Henri Nouwen, Christian priest and author, suggested that these stripes are rooted in five lies about our identity:[10]

1. **I am what I have.**
   Our self-worth is tied to our material possessions and our wealth—the outward signs that assure us of our value because we doubt we have any without them.
2. **I am what I do.**
   We judge ourselves by our accomplishments and productivity, feeling that we are only valuable when we are useful.

3. **I am what other people say or think about me.**
   We see ourselves through the eyes of others and become people-pleasers and chameleons who morph to become what others want us to be. We are devastated when we don't gain their approval.

4. **I am nothing more than my worst moment.**
   We spiral into shame and self-flagellation for our mistakes and become trapped by self-hatred, doubt, and helplessness. We sabotage ourselves because we don't believe we are worthy of good things.

5. **I am nothing less than my best moment.**
   This self-aggrandizement is rooted in fear as we refuse to acknowledge our weaknesses and failures. We buy into the myth of our idealized self and ride on the coattails of our past successes instead being open to growth and accountability.

I have believed every single one of these lies. I allowed them to define and distort my sense of self. From an early age, I discovered that I could get positive attention and affirmation for my accomplishments. I became a classic overachiever, striving to be the best at everything I attempted and scared to death of failure. There was one time during my sophomore year in high school when my mom accompanied me to a meeting with the school counselor. She pressed him about why I wasn't ranked first in my class despite getting straight A's. When the counselor explained that the extra class I was taking actually lowered my grade point average, my mom complained about the injustice of it all. I learned that doing my best didn't really count unless others acknowledged that I was the best.

I carried these lies into my parenting, using my children's behavior as a barometer for how I was faring as a person and parent from day to day. When they threw themselves on the sidewalk and drew the disapproving stares of the 爷爷奶奶 (elderly men and women) with their earsplitting screams, I threatened to never take them outside again. When they were praised for sitting quietly and attentively during a meeting despite being only 2 and 4 years old, I patted myself on the back for training them so well. I didn't realize that I was perpetuating these lies of conditional love, allowing my relationship with them to be defined by what they did or didn't do, their best and worst moments.

Exposing these beliefs as falsehoods empowers us to reject them and replace them with truth. As we look in the mirror and beyond our stripes—the prerequisites we need to fulfill, the hoops we need to jump through, and the conditions we need to meet in order to feel worthy of love and belonging—we learn to see ourselves more clearly and compassionately. We begin to accept ourselves as we really are. Without all the posturing. Without all the performing. Without automatically defaulting to the patterns we learned from our pain. We can begin to put aside the stripes of our false selves, reject the lies, and return to our true selves.

CHAPTER 2

ACCEPTING OURSELVES

Seeing ourselves without our stripes can feel scary and vulnerable. We're like the emperor parading before the crowds in his beautiful new robes, only to be told he's actually naked. Our stripes are all a facade, but who are we without them? We feel naked and exposed.

In big ways and small, we grew up believing that our true selves were not welcome in the world. We were too loud, too quiet, too sensitive, too aggressive, too shy, too flighty. Too much, and yet not enough.

I'm just beginning to grieve all the ways that my true self was not honored and accepted as a child. When I was a little girl, I was the object of much affection because I was, frankly, adorable. My chubby arm rolls, crooked smile, and crescent eyes made all the aunties and uncles at church want to just eat me up. But being an introverted and sensitive child, I was often intimidated by all the gushing and grabbing. I didn't enjoy being forcibly taken away from my mother and passed around, pinched playfully, or having all eyes on me. I soon earned the nickname "No 小姐" or Little Miss No.

No, I do not want to give him a hug.
No, I do not want to go to the class alone.
No, I do not want to play piano for our guests.

Unfortunately, my "no's" were not often respected. Instead, I was told to be friendlier, to talk louder, to lighten up. I forced myself to behave in ways that went against my nature, seeing my disposition as inherently flawed, as something that needed to be fixed. I internalized the judgments of others. I believed that I was not loved as I was.

I'm still in a place of rediscovering and accepting myself. That place of woundedness, rejection, and masquerading is slowly becoming a place of healing as I learn to see my true nature as my gift rather than my shame.

Most of us have received messages of unworthiness. We've been taught to see ourselves through the lens of judgment, shame, and conditional love. But shame is a kind of self-flagellation—a contempt that we turn inward upon ourselves as punishment; a motivation to improve our ability to perform or conceal. Shame only adds more stripes to our backs.

In contrast, acceptance brings healing as we embrace our whole selves, not just the parts we present to the public for consumption. Learning to accept ourselves means we have to strip off the lens of shame and see instead with eyes of compassion: we are loved, just as we are.

This self-compassion gives us the courage to accept our imperfections. We can trust that when we don't meet our ideals, when we fail, when we feel inadequate, we are still loved and worthy of love. Being grounded in this truth empowers us to face our failings with humility and grace. We become less afraid to feel and express unpleasant emotions. We are more willing to take responsibility when we screw up. We learn to accept our humanity, that magical mix of perfect imperfection. Our identity is no longer rooted in our performance and we become freer.

Self-compassion also empowers us to accept our gifts. So much of our strength and unique contribution to the world was labeled as a weakness or shortcoming. We internalized those judgments, learning to water down our nature to make us more palatable. In doing so, we lost all our flavor. Learning to affirm our true selves means we can honor our essence instead of trying to hide it. We can celebrate the distinct tastes that each of us offers. Not everyone is meant to be sugary sweet. We need the salty, the tangy, the bitter, the spicy... all of it! Pure Iris extract.

This shift in perspective takes practice. As we sit with the discomfort of our naked truth, noticing our scars, our blemishes, and all the parts of ourselves we'd like to change, we will be tempted to return to the old way of seeing. We will default to that lens of shame and self-condemnation. When this happens—which it inevitably will—we can acknowledge it, recognize it for the carnival mirror that it is, and consciously choose compassion instead.

Seeing ourselves honestly and loving ourselves unconditionally is the only way we can show up authentically. It's the only way we can divest ourselves of our false tiger stripes. There's no shortcut, no way to bypass this important step in our untigering journey. Only when we offer that kind of radical acceptance to ourselves can we ever hope to offer it to our children.

CHAPTER 3

OWNING OUR STORIES

D espite our best untigering intentions, sometimes we find ourselves falling into the same patterns as our own parents. We make vows to parent differently, from minor pledges like, "I will never force my child to learn piano," to more bitter oaths like, "There's no way I will humiliate my daughter like my mother humiliated me." And yet, too often we put pressure on our kids to perform and succeed. We limit their freedoms for our convenience. We use shame and power (or worse) to get them to behave.

An important part of our healing journey involves us returning to our origin stories and reflecting on the ways we were parented. In order to make sense of where we are and where we are going, we have to look at where we've been.

Owning Your Story

Many of us have deep pain in our relationship with our parents. However pleasant things seem to be on the surface, underneath there may be distance, resentment, or even a sense of rejection. When we avoid attending to our childhood wounds, that unacknowledged pain and trauma festers and keeps us stuck. We end up reacting out of our past pain instead of responding to the present situation.

Brené Brown, in her book *Rising Strong*, wrote, "When we deny our stories, they define us. When we own our stories, we get to write a brave new ending."[11] We can take control of the narrative, but not until we own the story arc that has led us to where we are now.

My father was a stern and serious man who served in religious ministry his entire adult life. My childhood memories of him consist mostly of slaps to the hand, criticisms of my failures, and long periods of absence while he was away at meetings, conferences, trainings, and other church-related events. Sure, there were fun family vacations and laughter-filled afternoons playing soccer in the backyard, but I often felt that we, as his family, were an afterthought. It was a competition between us and work, and we always seemed to lose.

I remember the time when my older sister told my parents about her graduation baccalaureate ceremony. We all shrugged indifferently when my dad said he wasn't going to make it. It was just another in a long list of milestones, events, and occasions that he had missed. But on the day of the ceremony when her other classmates were surrounded by parents and extended family, my sister couldn't hide her disappointment and grief. I cried with her as we mourned how my dad had yet again chosen something else over us.

When Jason and I got married and started having children, I became very resentful whenever I was stuck at home while he would go out to play basketball or serve in church ministry. Even though I believed in the value of those activities, every time he pursued something outside of the family, I felt forgotten, unimportant, abandoned. I felt like the kids and I were not a priority. It wasn't until I connected it back to my relationship with my father that I realized I was reacting to a deeper pain. Unpacking that with Jason helped him to be more sensitive to my needs and helped me to be less insecure.

Naming our pain can rob it of its power. Ignoring our childhood wounds simply allows them to infect the rest of our lives, like it did in my marriage. Unprocessed trauma ends up leaking out in unhealthy ways, draining our life of energy, or destroying us from the inside out. In order to thoroughly clean out our wounds, we have to be willing to open them up and face the ugliness and messiness. We only prolong our own suffering if we don't.

I can't claim to know what this process will look like for you; it's so different for each individual. Some like to process internally by writing in a journal. Others need a trusted friend to talk to. Some may prefer support groups while others choose to see a therapist. A few brave ones may talk directly with their parents. For me, writing this book has been part of it. There are many ways to address our childhood wounds and heal our inner child, but whatever we do, we must own the pain that is part of our story.

Knowing Your Parents' Stories

My mom was born in Vietnam into an affluent Chinese family, the Vietnam War as the backdrop to her childhood. When she was just twelve, the tides turned when her father suddenly passed away. Her widowed mother, lacking the ability and emotional fortitude to provide for her family, pushed my mom to drop out of school and work in order to pay for her brothers' education. My mother, being an obedient firstborn daughter, found a job at a fabric factory. She spent the next few years there working 12 hour shifts on her feet, trying to scrape together enough money so that her family could eat more than just instant noodles.

My father was born in China to a wealthy businessman with two wives. He also experienced a reversal in fortune when the arrival of the Red Army forced his family to flee to Hong Kong. They moved into the refugee slums and were discriminated against by the locals.

There, my dad ran around with a gang of street boys and often got in trouble with his harsh father. Still, he was always the favored eldest son, born to the favored younger wife.

Like my parents, many children of that generation suffered war, poverty, displacement, family dysfunction, disease, and untimely death. They learned to function under patriarchal systems that demeaned women and dominated children. My youngest aunt was almost sold because my grandparents couldn't afford to raise another girl. Her older siblings had to weep and beg their parents to keep her. They all laugh about it now, but I can only imagine the deep wound that must have left, knowing that your own parents were willing and desperate enough to sell you. In such an environment, survival is the only goal. There is nothing left over for something as abstract as *love*.

My parents experienced further trauma in adulthood when they decided to move to the States. Leaving behind all they had known, they had to deal with the stress of living in a new culture, learning a new language, experiencing racism, and struggling to earn a livelihood. My father, who had come over to pursue a master's degree, had to take on a variety of odd jobs on top of a full course load. My mother, who graduated top of her college class in Hong Kong, had to care for her children and household in a completely foreign context without the support of extended family.

Knowing our parents' stories and their own complicated family histories can give us a clearer perspective of the challenges they faced and why they parented us as they did. Instead of simply blaming them for our pain, we can choose to understand the family trauma and social injustices that set the stage for their own stories. We can extend grace as we become more aware of our shared wounds. My mom and dad did the best they could to parent me with what they had, even when they were given so little. For that, I am immensely grateful.

I realize that not all of us are so fortunate to be reconciled with our parents. Accepting our parents doesn't mean we always need to let them into our lives. Part of acceptance may mean recognizing that they are unsafe and that we are not responsible for changing them. Especially as we parent the next generation and desire to break toxic generational patterns, strong boundaries may be appropriate to keep unhealthy cycles from being passed on. Estrangement from parents is heartbreaking, but its benefits can outweigh the pain. Some parents are so dysfunctional that they will suck us into their vortex of misery unless we escape their gravitational pull.

While there has been healing in my relationship with my parents, sometimes it's still hard to have heartfelt conversations and feel emotionally connected to them. Sometimes work and ministry still seem more of a priority to my dad than family. Sometimes I wonder if they even know me. But these things no longer affect me as deeply as they used to. I'm learning to release any expectations and just accept them and our relationship as it is. I no longer need them to tell me who I am.

Understanding our parents' stories may lead to forgiveness, strong boundaries, limited contact, or a complete cutting off of relationship. All these can be valid responses. Whatever we choose, we no longer need to let our parents' stories define the rest of our narrative. We can acknowledge how they shaped us, but then reclaim our own story.

Writing Your Ending

Writing our ending is a lifelong process of continual growth and self-awareness. As we process our past pain and grow into our true selves, we become less triggered by our past. As we change our self-talk and relationship with ourselves, we become more thoughtful in how we talk and relate to our children. Untigering starts with this inner work.

You can choose a mantra, prayer, word, song, or image to address a particular pain point. My friend Gretchen often reminds herself and others, "You are seen. You are known. You are loved." A healing word for me has been *delight*. It evokes a sense of joyful intimacy that I felt I lacked as a child who was driven by dutiful obedience. Noah carries around a lucky amethyst crystal in the shape of a heart to remind him that he is loved, whenever he feels anxious. Whatever we struggle with, we can find words, images, or tangible ways to rewrite the scripts imprinted on our minds and bodies.

What is a particular childhood wound you would like to address? What mantra, prayer, image, embodied practice, etc. can you choose to bring healing to that wound?

We can also lean on others in our healing. While our relationship with ourselves is integral, being a #selfhealer has not been my experience. Rather, I've found that relational violence, wounds, and isolation are healed by relational trust, love, and connection. We need others to help us relearn what it means to be in healthy relationships: respectful partners, trusted friends, wise elders, and our own children who teach us what true love actually means.

While we don't have to be defined by the way our stories began, we can't just skip to the end and read the happily-ever-after either. As my friend Jenn often says, "There are no shortcuts to growth!" We have to make daily (and often moment-by-moment) choices to change our stripes. We will do so imperfectly and inconsistently, but slowly and surely these incremental shifts will change the eventual arc of our stories and the stories of generations to come.

I'm already seeing it happening in my own family and it makes me hopeful about the remainder of my untigering story. And I'm hopeful about your story too.

Let's write a brave new ending together.

PART 2

REWIRING OUR INSTINCTS

Like all animals, tigers have a few survival instincts that kick in whenever faced with a threat: fight, flight, or freeze. However, being an apex predator, a tiger's primary instinct is not to cower or flee; it's to dominate.

In my early years of parenthood, I leaned heavily on my tiger-parenting instincts. My impulse was to subdue like the alpha predator I was. I'd snarl and roar. "You do NOT speak to me like that!" I'd threaten with bared fangs and sharpened claws. "You just lost the chance to play on the iPad, buddy!" I'd creep away in a huff. "I cannot handle you right now."

These are natural responses when we see the world as brutal and hostile. In order to survive in this unfriendly environment as children, we had to follow our fight-flight-freeze instincts. We became aggressive or ran away from conflict to protect ourselves. We shut down emotionally, became controlling, or hid our true selves to avoid uncomfortable feelings and situations. Unfortunately, we don't automatically outgrow these survival strategies. We bring them into our adulthood and parenting, believing that we must eat or be eaten. We view our relationships with our children and the world around us as adversarial and antagonistic.

But what may have served us in a hostile environment is now failing us in our attempts to create a safe and loving space for our children. Ruling over our children with domination and disrespect does not lay a healthy foundation for attachment and real relationship. No one likes to be controlled and tyrannized! Children know intuitively when they are not being honored and quickly lose respect for those who violate their dignity.

Although I don't consider myself inherently motherly or nurturing, I know that a lot of that is because I've had those natural instincts conditioned out of me. I was taught to compete, look out for number one, be self-sufficient, be invulnerable. But human beings are actually designed to love and be loved, to rely on one another, to build secure attachments with others. Rather than thinking that it goes against my nature, untigering is actually returning to my true self. It's reawakening that soft part of me that got hardened along the way.

In order to rewire our tiger parenting instincts, we have to recognize why they were necessary: they were our way of coping with the stresses we were exposed to as children. They protected us when we felt threatened. We can acknowledge how they served and sheltered us, then integrate them into our growth without allowing them to control us.

Elizabeth Gilbert, in her book *Big Magic: Creative Living Beyond Fear*, saw her fear in this way—not as something to be rejected and ignored, but as something to be invited along for the ride.

> Dearest Fear:
> I understand you'll be joining us [on this road trip], because you always do. I acknowledge that you believe you have an important job to do in my life, and that you take your job seriously. Apparently your job is to induce complete panic whenever I'm about to do anything interesting—and, may I say, you are superb at your job. So by all means, keep doing your job, if you feel you must. But I will also be doing my job on this road trip, which is to work hard and stay focused... I recognize and respect that you are part of this family, and so I will never exclude you from our activities, but still—your suggestions will never be followed. You're allowed to have a seat, and you're allowed to have a voice, but you are not allowed to have a vote. You're not allowed to touch the road maps; you're not allowed to suggest detours; you're not allowed to fiddle with the temperature. Dude, you're not even allowed to touch the radio. But above all else, my dear old familiar friend, you are absolutely forbidden to drive.[12]

While we can compassionately make room for our fear, that doesn't mean we need to give it the steering wheel. The survival mechanisms that kept us alive in our childhood don't help us to thrive as adults and parents. Reacting out of our triggers prevents us from fostering loving connections now that we are safe.

The good news is that while the fight-flight-freeze response is biologically hardwired within us, we can learn to calm it and rewire our brains to see and interpret our experiences differently.

Understanding Our Emotional Triggers

Lisa Feldman Barrett, professor of Psychology at Northeastern University and author of *How Emotions are Made: The Secret Life of the Brain*,[13] debunks the myth that our emotional reactions are built in: innate responses given to us at birth that are just waiting to get triggered by outside stimuli. Instead, they are built—through our brain's interpretation of the physical sensations in our bodies, in relation to what's going on in the world around us, and influenced by our culture, upbringing, and past experiences. In her TED Talk,[14] Barrett asserts that emotions are actually just "guesses"—predictions and anticipations that our brains construct. If a new mother feels anxious when she hears her baby cry, it's not because she's automatically triggered. It's because she is interpreting those cries to mean that her baby will be up all night, that she won't get enough sleep, that her partner is lazy and useless, that she is incompetent. She may not be aware that this is what's happening, but she is indeed imbuing meaning into those cries because of her past experiences and perceptions.

Barrett goes on to explain:

> Emotions which seem to happen to you are actually made by you. You are not at the mercy of mythological emotion circuits

which are buried deep inside some ancient part of your brain. You have more control over your emotions than you think you do...[Y]our brain is wired so that if you change the ingredients that your brain uses to make emotion, then you can transform your emotional life. So if you change those ingredients today, you're basically teaching your brain how to predict differently tomorrow, and this is what I call being the architect of your experience.

Understanding that we are the ones who construct our emotions empowers us to change the script inside our heads. When we feel emotionally overwhelmed and upset, we can take time to slow down and breathe, consciously noticing our physical sensations, our emotions, and the thoughts running through our minds. By bringing this awareness to our experience, we interrupt our automatic responses and calm our nervous system, allowing our higher-order thinking to work. Emotions are embodied experiences, and learning to regulate our bodies and minds is an essential part of managing our emotional "triggers."

Furthermore, we can learn to interpret our experiences differently, questioning the many false assumptions that we believe about our children, ourselves, and our world. Imagine you have made a delicious pot of congee and your child refuses to eat it, requesting macaroni and cheese instead. Rather than labeling them ungrateful and disobedient, consider the fact that there may be real sensory issues or physiological reasons behind their picky eating. How misguided it would be to punish a child when they are suffering and in need of our support! Or perhaps they won't eat because they are pushing back against our desire to control them. Maybe the problem would resolve itself if we didn't engage in the power struggle and they were able to exercise bodily autonomy. Adjusting our perspective to see with eyes of compassion rather than judgment can transform the way we feel and react to any given situation.

We can also curate new, positive experiences that help rewire our brain and inform our future predictions. The consistent love and acceptance of a friend or partner can challenge the belief that love is conditional. It reminds us that there can be safety and security in relationships. Finding a compassionate therapist or community can help us heal from our past pains so that we avoid projecting them onto our children.

While we are wired for self-protection and survival, we are also wired for connection and love. By bringing awareness to our triggers, we can tap into that nurturing intuition that is buried underneath our survival mechanisms. By trusting in the healing power of our bodies and the neuroplasticity of our brain, we can be hopeful in our ability to change. We are no longer children who are at the mercy of the adults in our lives. We are now the adults, and we have power to break the cycle for ourselves and the next generation.

This next section challenges different assumptions that many of us have internalized, giving us new interpretations that can rewire our brains and repair our relationships with our children.

CHAPTER 4

RETHINKING A CHILD'S NATURE

I t matters how we view children. Our beliefs about a child's essence determine how we interpret and respond to their behavior. Unfortunately, most of us are conditioned to see children in some pretty demeaning and damaging ways.

Children as Sinful

Influenced by puritanical religious teachings, many believe that children come into the world as inherently sinful, willful, lazy, foolish, and feral. Since we see a child's intrinsic nature as corrupt, it becomes our God-given duty to punish it and correct it.

The evil within must be driven out.
The obstinance must be broken.
The slothfulness must be disciplined.
The foolishness must be chastised.
The wildness must be tamed.

Such a view encourages us to resort to harsh and punitive measures. It teaches us to see our children through eyes of judgment and condemnation and creates a very unhealthy dynamic between parent and child.

Much of my own untigering experience has been a direct result of deconstructing these toxic religious beliefs that were rooted in shame and self-hatred. I stopped focusing on everything that was wrong with my kids and I began to see them through the eyes of unconditional love and grace. I stopped believing that they were degenerate, manipulative, or disobedient and I began trusting that their nature was wired for love, connection, safety, autonomy, and significance. Any "sinful" act on their part was simply their way of trying to get their needs met. When I reframed my kids' behavior in this way, I was able to empathize with them and work on meeting their needs. Punishing their behavior no longer made any sense, nor was it effective in teaching them more appropriate ways to address their needs. (I cover this more in the "Rethinking Misbehavior" chapter.)

Children as Innocent

While it's problematic to see children as inherently sinful, seeing children as pure and innocent can be harmful as well. It fails to recognize their full humanity, robbing them of their agency and excusing them from the natural consequences of their choices. Rather than placing moral judgment upon them, we can simply accept that children are just as capable of good and evil as adults are. Teresa Graham Brett, activist and author of *Parenting for Social Change*, reminds us, "If we can see children as the competent and complex human beings that they are, we can begin to see their behavior beyond the polarity of positive and negative. We can begin to see the nuances of who they are and how they see the world."[15]

Children as Empty

Some people imagine children to be empty containers—devoid of their own thoughts, opinions, or predispositions, and meant to be filled with whatever we deem appropriate. They are not seen as having their own legitimate needs, desires, thoughts, or agency. They are passive recipients of the knowledge and experiences that we carefully choose for them. But if we're honest with ourselves, we know that this is simply not true. We see it when one child giggles hysterically when tossed in the air, while another cries uncontrollably. We see it when one child loves quiet rainy days reading books on the sofa, while another loves running around and exploring the outdoors.

I won't get into the age-old debate of nature vs. nurture, but I do believe that children come into the world with their own essences and preferences. They are not vacuous vessels or shapeless clay just waiting for us to fill or mold them. They are their own masterpieces, waiting for us to discover and treasure them as they are. As Dr. Shefali Tsabary, acclaimed author, speaker, and clinical psychologist so vividly describes, a child is "a spirit throbbing with its own signature."[16] To believe that they are any less is dehumanizing. To believe that we can forge them into an image of our own making is arrogant.

Children as Extensions

In Chinese culture, children are seen as extensions of the family. Their actions and attitudes reflect upon the parents and community, bringing either honor or shame. They are not seen as singular or idiosyncratic, but as part of a greater whole. Because of this, there is immense pressure for a child to conform to social norms and values and any divergence or expression of individuality that goes against such norms is generally frowned upon.

While it may be tempting to react to suffocating cultural, social, and familial expectations by going to the opposite end of the spectrum, what we need is not hyper-individualism but healthy boundaries. This means negotiating the tension between our separateness and our togetherness as parent and child. We can honor our child's individuality and autonomy while still grounding them in their place in the family, culture, and greater society. The "me" and the "we" don't have to threaten each other when we make room for both. The problems arise when parents become a colonizing force and subsume the child's identity into their own. As untigering parents, we must resist this unhealthy impulse.

Children as Inferior

Yet another view of children sees them as less than full persons, undeserving of all the dignity and rights that we extend to each other as adults. We dehumanize them every time we invalidate their perspectives and feelings, ignore their needs, violate their boundaries, control them for the sake of our convenience, rob them of their autonomy, or speak disrespectfully to them. We see them as unable to bear the responsibility of freedom and respect, so we justify our inhumane treatment of them. We regard them as subordinate, so we literally label them "*minors.*"

This adultist view of children is pervasive and unquestioned in much of society, yet it is something that should very much be interrogated and challenged. It is unacceptable that we do to children what we would never do to other adults or allow to be done to us as adults. We need to begin to shift the cultural perspective and start seeing children as whole persons who are worthy of love, respect, and dignity, whatever their age. (I address this further in the chapter "Checking our Adultism.")

Children as Adults

Others treat children like miniature adults, expecting children to behave in ways that are convenient for the adult world—quiet, calm, attentive, rational, and self-controlled. Such a view ignores the realities of brain development and human psychology. Big emotions, an abundance of energy, and a lack of self-control are all perfectly natural for children as they continue to mature and figure out how to navigate their world. By not allowing children to be children, we communicate a lack of acceptance and understanding. Our children feel straitjacketed, learning to tamp down their normal instincts in order to appease adults.

We must understand that—physically, emotionally, cognitively, hormonally—a child does not yet have the ability or resources to act like an adult. Rather than having this unrealistic expectation, we can learn to accept whatever developmental stage our child is in. We can understand their limits and need for support. We can adjust our expectations to be developmentally appropriate. We can stop projecting onto them our adult standards and learn to accept them as they are in the present moment.

Many of us don't even realize that we have these beliefs about children. They may be unconscious assumptions we have based on what we've observed and experienced in our society, culture, and family. However, when our gut reaction toward children is to control and dominate them, it's a signal that our beliefs need to change. While I admit that I am still influenced by these distorted perspectives and expectations, I'm trying to unlearn these false narratives and re-educate myself.

What do you believe about a child's nature? Take time to articulate what you truly believe about children. Then evaluate those beliefs. Are they based on reality, or on false assumptions? What is the end result of those beliefs? Do they empower you to treat your children with more love, respect, and empathy? Or do they provoke dominance, frustration, disappointment, and rage?

Rather than focusing on trying to change our treatment of children, we need to get to the root—our beliefs. When we change our false perceptions and question our unfair judgments—learning to honor our children's wholeness and humanity—our tiger instinct to punish, yell, demean, or control them no longer feels right. We can disrupt our reactive behaviors by consciously naming and re-forming our beliefs.

CHAPTER 5

RETHINKING A PARENT'S ROLE

I grew up in a household where there was a strict hierarchy—typical for traditional Chinese families built on authoritarianism, patriarchy, and 孝 (filial piety). My paternal grandfather was the patriarch, with my dad next in line, the womenfolk under him, and us children down at the bottom. The older generation was given all the keys to power and privilege while the children were expected to obey without question. I often felt like a peon, rushing around to follow the orders that my dad or grandfather barked at us from their comfortable seats on the sofa. I'd set the table, weed the garden, practice piano, or whatever else I was asked to do, not because I really honored my parents, but because I knew the harsh punishment I would incur if I didn't. On the surface, I was a compliant child, but underneath I was always simmering with resentment.

If, as children, we are subject to this kind of disempowerment, when we become adults and have children of our own, we often expect the tables to turn. *We* should now have the right to those keys. We want to express ourselves and have our needs met in ways that were ignored in our childhood. We expect our kids to fall in line and wait their turn. Now that we are the parents, we view our role as the authority, the leader, the one responsible for making sure our child turns out well.

We. Know. Best.

Apparently, our kids didn't get the memo. They let us know in no uncertain terms that they are their own people. It can be very triggering and upsetting when our own children refuse to participate in the hierarchy that we were forced to submit to.

I remember one time when we were visiting our close friends in Thailand and they invited us out to a meal. We were finishing up dinner at the restaurant when Caleb, my youngest child, straight up announced out loud, "I'm still hungry. Can I get dessert?"

I was mortified.

He had pretty much violated every rule of Asian etiquette! How embarrassing that he would openly dare to *want* something.

Thankfully, instead of being offended, our gracious hosts commended him for speaking up and making his wishes known. They celebrated his sense of power and self-awareness. And then they ordered him a big bowl of mango with black sticky rice and coconut milk.

I thought about why Caleb's request made me feel so uncomfortable, even though it was spoken without entitlement or guile. I realized that, in contrast to my son, I never would have dreamed of asking for dessert as a child. Growing up, *I never knew I was allowed to want anything.* I had to make myself small and invisible to accommodate adult expectations. I wasn't allowed to express my authentic self. Seeing Caleb freely do so with such confidence that night was embarrassing, but inspiring as well.

Once we begin to change the way we see children, we begin to change our perspective on what our parental responsibility is. We realize that our goal should not be to mold them into a person of our own making—someone in our own likeness or one who fits society's expectations. Rather, it's to provide them with unconditional love and unwavering support, empowering them to fulfill their *own* goals and dreams. Sure, we may have more experience, more knowledge of the world, and hopefully more wisdom to pass on. But we must be careful to honor our child's own path.

The following are some ways to reimagine our parental role.

Model

When we see ourselves as models, we focus on managing ourselves rather than our children. We try to set an example for the attitudes and actions that we hope to see in our children, knowing that actions speak louder than words. More than simply giving commands and issuing directives, we do the hard work of embodying the values we claim to possess. We give generously, speak respectfully, forgive quickly, defend boldly. This is the true work of the parent—to become our best selves.

Children are quick to notice the hypocrisy when we ourselves do not do what we ask of them. When we yell at our children to stop yelling, or tell them to take a break from their screens when we've been binge-watching Netflix all day, our double standards are exposed and we lose credibility. I remember the time my grandfather chewed me out for having my elbows on the table during dinnertime. I obediently tucked my arms to my side, sufficiently chastised, only to see him putting his own elbows on the table a few minutes later! I didn't dare to point it out to him, but I never forgot it. It was such an insignificant matter, and yet it made me deeply distrustful of adults who told me one thing but did another.

Being a model means holding ourselves to our own standards, but it also means recognizing our inability to do so consistently! Knowing that we often fail to meet our own ideals can give us compassion for our children and ourselves. There is room to make mistakes and grow together. We are all in process.

Gardener

John Holt, author, educator, and proponent of unschooling wrote this about an adult's role in a child's life: "We can think of ourselves not as teachers but as gardeners. A gardener does not grow flowers; he tries to give them what he thinks they need and they grow by themselves."[17] In other words, we cannot compel our kids to become who we want them to be by sheer willpower. Instead, we trust that our children have within themselves that seed of life—that innate capacity to grow, problem-solve, and seek ways to survive and thrive. All they need from us is the support, protection, encouragement, and resources so that they can, indeed, "grow by themselves."

Each type of plant requires different amounts of water, nutrients, and sunshine. We cannot force an orchid to be like a dandelion, nor can we coerce spring flowers to bloom year-round. Instead, a good gardener understands the nature and needs of each plant and seeks to provide a healthy environment for its development. We don't need to bend our child's will or go against their natural inclinations, acting like carpenters who work the wood to create our own vision. We simply need to foster their organic growth.

In China, the markets sometimes sell fruits and vegetables that resemble little Buddhas, soccer balls, or hearts. While the fruit is still growing, a plastic mold is placed around it so that the fruit is forced to grow into the shape of the mold. Such gardening resembles the domineering tiger parenting that confines children to conform to a preconceived image. It doesn't allow for the child to develop naturally. In fact, it inhibits their growth. Growing square watermelons to fit into tiny fridges may be convenient and entertaining for us, but when it comes to children, it shows a lack of acceptance. It dishonors their nature and autonomy. As parents, we need to communicate to our children that they are unconditionally loved and accepted as they are. Being a gardener means supporting our children in being themselves, not in being who *we* want them to be.

Coach

A coach is someone who helps you hone specific skills to reach your goals. It is someone who facilitates learning by providing resources, training, and instruction. The etymology of the word "coach" comes from the literal idea of a coach as a vehicle of transport, carrying the student from where they are to their desired destination. Unfortunately, we tiger parents are too often transporting our kids to where they don't want to go. They have not consented to come along for the ride! Instead of a coach, we function more like a train conductor who already has a predetermined schedule and terminus, sending our kids off to SAT prep classes, violin lessons, and basketball camps, whether they like it or not!

Now there is nothing wrong with upskilling per se, but this should be done by following the child's lead, not by imposing our own expectations or definitions of success. A good question to ask ourselves is if our child would choose to do this activity without any motivation or intervention on our part. Is it an expression of an intrinsic desire or interest, or are they doing it because of the pressure or desire to please us?

Being a coach means that we also need to be careful about the feedback we give to our child. If our child enjoys drawing but is not interested in improving their skills, let them just doodle and play. There is no need for them to receive instruction if they don't want it, even if we see how much they could improve if they only had a little guidance. That is our own ego talking, and doesn't reflect the child's own interests. When we give critical feedback and unsolicited advice, we rob them of the joy they experience in their creative expression. Our "coaching" can make them self-conscious as they become aware of being evaluated and pushed to perform.

Functioning as a coach requires us to respect and listen to our children. Instead of viewing yourself as a leader and director, try taking on the supporting and empowering role of coach.

Guide

I've also heard that respectful parents act as guides. Our children are like newcomers to a foreign country. As local inhabitants familiar with the cultural norms of the land, we can provide our children with wisdom and guidance. Because we have more experience and understanding of how things work, we can help these newcomers stay safe, understand expectations, communicate well, and learn how to thrive in this society.

This is not to say that we should be like one of those pushy tour guides who forces you to wear a group tour shirt, herds you through ten scenic spots in a day, and guilts you into buying a souvenir at the jade factory. A good guide is one who is informative but not coercive. We can point out things of interest and warn of potential dangers, but our job is to educate, not to control.

People often assume that peaceful parenting means that we allow children to run wild and behavior to go unchecked. But untigering is not unparenting. We have a role to play as parents; it's just that that role need not include coercion and control. We do have authority and power and responsibility, but instead of using them in an authoritarian way, we can share those privileges and use them to serve and empower our children. We can model, nurture, protect, coach, influence, and guide.

There are many ways to relate to our children as parents without being oppressive. We just have to have the courage and creativity to imagine new roles that are rooted in respect.

CHAPTER 6

RETHINKING MISBEHAVIOR

There are certain words we use to describe our kids when they act out. We call them naughty, disobedient, misbehaving. In Chinese, we use phrases like 淘气, 调皮, 不听话.

The interesting thing about these words is that we pretty much only use them when talking about children. We don't apply these to adults who behave badly. We use them to express our disappointment and displeasure when *children* don't comply with *adult* expectations. Terms like "naughty" and "misbehaving" actually reveal how so much of our parenting is built on parental power and preference.

The idea of misbehavior causes us to react with punishment and control. We resort to behavior management instead of understanding the heart motivations. It's like trying to drive a fever down instead of recognizing it as our immune system at work. When we see fevers as our bodies' natural response to an infection, they become helpful signals with a purposeful function, killing off pathogens and increasing white blood cell production. Likewise, we don't have to label certain behaviors as "bad." Instead, we can reframe these behaviors as valid responses to what's going on within them and around them.

That is exactly what Dr. Thomas Gordon, clinical psychologist and founder of Gordon Training International, proposed: **"Children don't misbehave, they simply behave to get their needs met."**[18] Everything our kids do, they do to get a need met, whether it's nourishment, nurturing, or someone to notice them. They are not out to push our buttons and make life difficult for us, however much evidence we have to the contrary. They are simply doing what is necessary to try to meet their needs for survival, safety, belonging, significance, and personal power.

This compassionate view teaches us to withhold judgment (and therefore, punishment) and consider what needs our child might be trying to satisfy. We can look beneath the surface to what might be driving the behavior. The grouchiness may be due to the lack of rest from last night's sleepover. The aggression on the playground may be coming from a place of fear. Oftentimes, the undesirable behavior can be resolved after a snack is eaten, a nap is taken, or a hug is given. Other times, there's a deeper problem that takes a longer time to heal; trust and connection need to be established before any change is seen. Either way, the parent's role is to help the child to get their needs met in appropriate and acceptable ways.

Punishing or scolding a child for their behavior fails to meet these underlying needs. It teaches them to either find sneakier ways to fulfill their needs, or to suppress their needs altogether. We can create compliant children this way—strong-arming them into obedience through fear—but we will never have their hearts. Rethinking misbehavior requires us to stop dividing behaviors into good and bad. By framing **all** behaviors as attempts to get needs met, we can begin to approach our kids with understanding and compassion instead of judgment and control. We can teach them to express themselves in ways that more effectively achieve their goals, solve their problems, and fulfill their needs.

Class Bully or Anxious Child?

When Caleb was in kindergarten, I attended a parent-teacher conference, expecting to hear a glowing report about how sweet and smart he was. Imagine my dismay when the teacher informed me that he had, in fact, been hitting and biting the other kids.

My immediate response was a mix of disbelief, embarrassment, and shame. *How could my adorable baby boy be the class bully?* I started wracking my brain for consequences severe enough to curb his aggressive behavior. By the time I left the meeting, I was ready to march straight home and teach Caleb a lesson about violence. Maybe a stern lecture and some expressions of disappointment would make him see the error of his ways.

But the more I thought about it, the more I wondered why he would physically lash out at kindergarten when he rarely did so at home. What was driving his aggression? Then, it came to me. He was spending hours away from home when he was accustomed to being by my side all day. He was in a Chinese-speaking environment when English was his first language. He probably didn't always understand what was going on, nor could he always effectively communicate his needs or boundaries. He wasn't mean; he was *stressed.*

When I talked with Caleb later that evening, I asked him about how he felt about kindergarten. He confirmed my suspicions, tearfully admitting that he was having a hard time. I empathized with him. Then we discussed different ways to get his needs met. We practiced some Chinese phrases he could use, rehearsed different scenarios, and talked about how to ask a teacher for help. Instead of punishing him for his "misbehavior," I was able to understand the reasons behind it and coach him with more effective and acceptable methods.

When we stop seeing our child's off-track behavior as willful disobedience and are able to identify the underlying needs they're trying to meet, we are more able to get to the root of the problem and help them. Instead of reacting to their behavior, we can learn to play detective and be compassionately curious about what is going on underneath the surface. We can slow down and ask ourselves the question, "What need is my child trying to meet?"

This is especially necessary when our kids don't have the cognitive or verbal skills to communicate their needs or emotions to us. They might not even know why they are acting out. In the above situation with Caleb, he probably wouldn't have been able to articulate his anxiety if I hadn't brought it up with him. We as parents have to learn to ask good questions, give children the vocabulary to describe their experiences, and be good interpreters of their behavior so that we can support them appropriately.

Let's stop branding our kids as bad, naughty, or misbehaving. Let's excise those labels from our vocabulary. Let's empathize with our children's hearts rather than evaluate them by their actions. There are truly no such things as bad kids—only kids who are trying to get their needs met.

CHAPTER 7

RETHINKING CORRECTION

Your child is crying, or screaming, or hitting. Or all of the above.

It takes all your willpower to not cry, scream, or hit back, but you can't just let this kind of behavior slide. You reach around for other parenting tools to get your kids to behave. When they get out of bed for the umpteenth time, you give them a consequence. When they hit their baby sister, you send them to their room. When they don't do their chores, you take away a privilege. And if you are a recovering tiger mom like me, you probably do all that with eyes glaring and teeth baring.

For years, I used such punitive measures to try to correct my kids' behavior. Noah used to have meltdowns so often that we were at our wits' end. None of our attempts to deal with his outbursts seemed to be working. We'd leave him alone to calm down, charge him money for locking the door, take away the items that he had thrown, or talk with him about how he was making bad choices. But the next day, he would just flip his lid again.

Once, we were working on a math worksheet during our homeschooling time (a familiar recipe for disaster in our household). I could see that he was getting frustrated and I was getting frustrated at his frustration. In the past, he had thrown books or written on the table, but this time he grabbed the mug of tea beside me and poured it out on the table. Without flinching, I snatched the mug out of his hands and dumped the remaining contents on his head. It guess that was my version of natural consequences!

Obviously, I needed help. I was fighting fire with fire and it was exhausting. I was getting to the point of helplessness.

The Problem with Correction

Correction seems like a good thing; and it can be. We don't want to be neglectful or permissive parents who do nothing when we see our kids go off course. But when we jump straight to fixing behavior without first connecting with our children, we actually shoot ourselves in the foot.

Dr. Jane Nelsen, author, and founder of Positive Discipline, has this to say about correction without connection:

> Extensive research shows that we cannot influence children in a positive way until we create a connection with them. It is a brain (and heart) thing. Sometimes we have to stop dealing with the misbehavior and first heal the relationship. Connection creates a sense of safety and openness. Punishment, lecturing, nagging, scolding, blaming or shaming create fight, flight, or freeze.[19]

Correction is actually counter-productive when we apply it without connection. It stimulates our child's reactive impulses, making it difficult to activate their higher-level, thinking brain. Over time, harsh correction and control can actually affect the child's brain development, making them more prone to fear, anger, addiction, or anxiety.[20] As I learned more about peaceful parenting and the research behind it, I realized how my punitive parenting methods were actually contributing to my son's meltdowns. **What he needed was not more correction, but more connection.**

Too often, I had abandoned him to deal with his overwhelming emotions on his own instead of being a calming presence. Too often, I had given him a consequence instead of offering compassion. Too often, I had walked away at the slightest hint of his frustration instead of sticking around to provide help.

I decided to change my M.O. The next time my son got upset, I went into the bedroom and sat with him. At first, he refused to answer me when I asked him what was wrong. He shrugged me off when I tried to rub his back. He batted my hand away when I offered a hug. I was tempted to leave. It was obvious he didn't want me there, and I could feel my own temper rising.

But then, a small miracle happened. He began to inch his way over to me. He leaned up against me. He nudged himself under my arm. And then he finally melted into my lap. We spent the next few minutes talking about what he was feeling. I listened to him and connected with him physically and emotionally. Over the next few days, weeks, and months, I tried to connect with him whenever he had a meltdown. Sometimes, I just couldn't do it. I would be too triggered and angry. I knew that I would say or do something I'd regret, so I just had to remove myself and cool off. But when the opportunity inevitably presented itself, I'd try again.

I would hold my son.

I would hold my tongue.

I would hold his big emotions and give space for them.

I would try to connect more and correct less. And I found that the more I connected, the less I actually needed to correct.

The Heart of Connection

A sense of belonging and connection is a basic desire and goal for us as humans. When our children lack a strong sense of belonging and don't receive enough positive attention from us, they behave in attention-seeking ways. To them, even bad attention is better than no attention. In contrast, when our kids feel connected to us, they become safe and secure in our love. They don't feel compelled to act out in negative ways because we're already giving them the connection they need. Often, by simply taking the time to proactively connect with our kids, the undesirable behavior naturally decreases. For my son, the change was not immediate, but it was noticeable.

Slowly, he started to:

- have fewer outbursts.
- have the capacity to handle more frustration.
- recover more quickly after a meltdown.
- ask me for what he needed emotionally.

The more effort I put into connecting with him, the less correcting I had to do. My connection with him actually helped him become more receptive and regulated. Dr. Nelsen reminds us, **"Children do better when they feel better."** This feels counterintuitive to tiger parents who somehow believe that children do better when we make them feel bad for what they've done. But no amount of lecturing or correcting helped my son more than my loving and empathic responses.

This may be very foreign to many of us. Few of us have grown up with affectionate and attuned parents who understood our hearts. It may feel unnatural and awkward to talk about deep feelings and hurts with our children when that was never modeled for us. But our children need us to break the cycle and start learning new patterns. We can offer open arms instead of pointed fingers, words of understanding instead of harsh criticisms, connection instead of isolation. It's going to take practice to rewire our instincts, but don't give up. Push through the discomfort and, in time, it will get easier, even if it never gets *easy*.

(I give some practical action items in the "Building Connection" chapter.)

A Time for Correction?

Is there ever a time for correction? Absolutely.

We do our children a disservice if we let them run amok without boundaries or guidance. But correction should always be done in the context of connection.

Dr. Bruce Perry,[21] a leading expert on childhood trauma, offers a helpful sequence for how to activate our child's learning brain so that they can make better choices and learn from their mistakes.

Regulate $\implies$ Relate $\implies$ Reason

We often want to jump straight to correcting a behavior, without realizing that a child cannot effectively reason when they are dysregulated and disconnected. Their "reptilian brain" (the brain stem that governs survival instincts) and "mammalian brain" (the limbic system that governs their emotions) are overstimulated, and the logical part of their brain goes off-line. In order to help them learn and reflect on their choices, we must take the time to calm and attune to our child. Only then can their brains be settled enough to activate the rational prefrontal cortex so that they can reason and change their behavior. Understanding this neurobiology teaches us to be a calming and empathetic presence for our kids rather than one that is critical and chastising.

Even then, reasoning together looks more like coaching than correcting. Correction implies a top-down approach, with the parent being the one with all the answers. Sure, a parent can just preach to a child, but a much more meaningful way to learn is for the child to be given a chance to self-reflect, problem solve, and draw their own lessons. Gently guiding, modeling, and coaching are respectful ways that we can influence our children and share our wisdom without using our power over them.

CHAPTER 8

RETHINKING CONTROL

We all want children who are self-controlled and self-regulated. Unfortunately, most of us assume that the way to reach that goal is through *parental* control and *parental* regulation.

At least that's what I had assumed.

When my boys were young, I managed their sleep schedules, vegetable consumption, sugar intake, screen times, clothing choices, and homework standards. But what I ended up with was a grand total of one controlling mommy and zero self-controlled children! This became evident when, one day, I found out that they had stashed vitamins in their bunk bed. They had been so starved for taboo sweets that even gummy vitamins were worth hoarding. I was trying to teach them moderation and responsibility through micro-management, and I was clearly failing.

Contrary to popular belief, strictness and deprivation don't lead to self-control. They lead to over-indulgence. They lead to a lack of personal boundaries and responsibility. Dr. Mai Stafford, a researcher at the University College London who led a study on the long-term effects of parenting on wellbeing, states: "Psychological control can limit a child's independence and leave them less able to regulate their own behaviour."[22] In other words, **children who are always ruled and restricted by parents don't know how to rule themselves.** When the locus of control is always outside of themselves, they never get the chance to manage their own impulses or exercise their own will. Such children may seem well-behaved and disciplined, but the minute they are out from under their parents' thumbs, they often go wild.

Just look at the effects of strict parenting in our own lives. We like to have a sugary beverage with every meal out because as kids we were only ever allowed to order water. We're obsessed with the latest movies because our parents never allowed us to go to the theater. We indulge our desire for the latest gadget because our parents never bought them for us. We end up in unhealthy relationships behind our parents' backs because they forbade us to date.

Or maybe that's just me.

But it seems apparent that those of us who were raised by strict parents grow up trying to compensate for what we were deprived of in our childhoods. We develop unhealthy appetites for the very things that were withheld from us. It's human nature, after all, to want what you can't have.

Strict tiger parenting may therefore lead to controlled children, but not necessarily *self*-controlled children... or adults.

So what's the answer?

Freedom Fosters Self-Control

Imagine having buffet... every single day.

Like any good Asian who wants to get their money's worth, you probably start off bingeing on all the sushi, prime rib, and crab legs. You stay away from the salad bar and bread that will waste your precious gastric real estate. But you still circle back for an assortment of little cakes and ice cream. There's always room for dessert.

This doesn't go on forever, however. Eating like that every day for breakfast, lunch, and dinner is not sustainable. At some point—a few days, weeks, or even months into this initial stage of reckless consumption—you reach an equilibrium. Instead of sampling everything or piling your plate precariously high, you learn to take only the things that your body is craving. You stop when you are satisfied rather than gorging yourself like an overstuffed dumpling. Even though you *could* eat all you want, you don't. You realize it just makes you feel gross. You're able to stop because whatever you want will always be there tomorrow. This is a picture of how freedom can actually foster self-control.

Giving children the autonomy to listen to their bodies, have their own preferences, and practice making decisions helps them to exercise their self-control muscle. When we place arbitrary limits on our kids, they often make unwise choices in an attempt to resist our control and exercise their personal power. When we honor their freedom and bodily autonomy, they learn to respond rather than react, paying attention to the situation and how they're feeling physically and emotionally. We can constantly remind our kids, *"Listen to your body."*

When the locus of control is in their hands, they practice making choices that are appropriate for them personally and begin to recognize the actual benefits and consequences of those choices. *"Hmm, eating all that White Rabbit candy sort of made me feel sick. Maybe I'll just have two next time."* They grow to discern rather than blindly obey. *"Tomorrow is Saturday and I can sleep in, so maybe I can stay up now and finish this game of Exploding Kittens."* They take more responsibility because they are the ones making the decision. *"I want to bring a book to read at the restaurant, so I'll pack it in my backpack."*

This buffet of choices and freedoms allows our kids to learn through trial and error. The hard part is for us parents not to intervene and micromanage at every turn, especially when we observe a lot of errors going on. We can always give our input and advice, but just as we would honor the autonomy of another adult, we have to be willing to let our kids make mistakes. If we don't, we rob them of the learning opportunities that natural consequences provide.

Of course, there's a caveat. I'm not saying that anything goes. This metaphorical buffet should not allow strychnine in the food or rats in the kitchen. Babies should not be given steak knives or hard liquor. The environment needs to be safe, supportive, and developmentally appropriate for your child. Kids with sensory issues may need more routine and limits. Those who've experienced trauma or scarcity may be overwhelmed by too many choices or feel the impulse to hoard. Provide them with freedom and choice, but in wise and loving ways that only you and your child can define together. No matter their specific needs, I still believe it is never our job to control our kids. Instead, we can control the environment so that they can practice their autonomy in ways that are safe and responsible.

My partner and I have been putting this theory of freedom into practice for a few years now. We used to put our boys down to bed religiously at 7:30 pm. Truth be told, it was more for our sanity than for their well-being, but when we realized that enforcing a strict bedtime didn't teach them to be in tune with their own bodies, we backed off. We let them decide their own bedtimes. At first, we'd find them staying up past ten o'clock, bleary eyed but intent on seeing how far they could push the limit. We'd suggest getting some rest but ultimately respected their bodily autonomy, saying goodnight and heading off to sleep while they stayed up reading or playing. After a while, they stopped reacting to the imagined limit and started turning their attention to what actually felt good for them. Noah would announce that he was tired and head off to bed on his own. Caleb would take a nap in the middle of the day if he felt tired. We found that with time, patience, support, and respectful guidance, they were completely capable of controlling themselves.

We have applied this to every aspect of their lives, from food, to clothing, to screen time, to hygiene. (I go into more detail about this in the "Bodily Autonomy" chapter.)

What results have we noticed in our kids as we've honored their bodily autonomy?

- Increased self-control as they are less tempted by "forbidden fruit."
- Fewer power struggles and complaints because they have decision-making power and buy-in.
- Critical thinking skills as they talk through what choices make the most sense.

Sooner or later, our kids will grow up and have access to the king of all buffets: **adulthood.** They will choose when to sleep (and who to sleep with), what to eat (and how much to drink), what to watch (and who to listen to). We can make all their decisions for them now and hope that they'll grow up to make good ones themselves. Or we can trust them with freedom now under our loving guidance.

I don't know about you, but I'm choosing the buffet.

CHAPTER 9

RETHINKING EMOTIONS

Culturally, the Chinese are not known for their effusive exuberance or emotional outbursts. My family was fairly typical in this regard. My father was a serious man; my sister, brother, and I learned to discern whether he was amused or displeased by the ever-so-slight difference in the angle of his lips. A 2° angle up or down could determine whether the answer to a request would be yes or no. A dispassionate "Not bad" was the equivalent of him doing backflips. A flaring of the nostrils, raising of the eyebrows, or narrowing of the eyes was all it took to scare me into submission.

Conversations were limited to the basics: homework, health, and household responsibilities.

> 作业做好了吗？ *Have you finished your homework?*
> 你上火了。多喝一点儿水。 *You have too much "heat" in your body. Drink more water.*
> 把你的衣服收起来 ！ *Put away your clothes!*

I can barely remember a time when I discussed with my parents anything related to my inner life. Tantrums were not tolerated, weepiness was scorned, over-excitement was frowned upon, anxiety was derided. I was so unaccustomed to displays of strong emotion that they made me very uncomfortable. I would want to escape them or smother them whenever they arose, whether it was in myself or in others.

Unsurprisingly, I internalized the belief that emotions were irrelevant; that they were signs of weakness; that they exposed my vulnerability to predators out there who would sniff me out and take me down. I learned to shut down any big emotions on either end of the spectrum, choosing to modulate within the range of what was pleasant and presentable.

Unfortunately, that was no way to be human.

When I had kids and discovered that, human as they were, they refused to follow suit and tamp down their big emotions, I would feel very triggered. I still do.

Just the other day, Jason and the kids were putting together our new trampoline. It had already been a frustrating morning after a little mistake had meant they had to undo and redo a whole step. Then, right when they were about to finish, they noticed that the net was not attached to the poles properly and had to be fixed. Apparently, that was the last straw, because Noah rage-quit and walked off. I was so annoyed. *Why does everything have to be such a big deal?* I wanted to go after him and yell, "Come back out here, young man!" but thankfully had the presence of mind to shut up and cool off. When Noah eventually returned on his own, I was about to break out into a lecture when Jason walked over to him and gently put his arm around him. He empathized with how Noah felt and encouraged him to push through, even when things were hard. I was humbled. Looking at Jason and Noah at that moment was a sweet reminder of how to hold space for our children's emotions.

While emotions still feel somewhat foreign and uncomfortable for me, I'm slowly getting back in touch with my humanity. I'm trying to name my feelings and make room for them. I'm starting to pause and listen to what they're trying to tell me instead of ignoring them. Here are some lessons I've been learning along the way.

Feelings Are Meant to be Felt

Feelings are meant to be felt. Mind-blowing, I know. But what seems so obvious is actually an instinct that we have to reawaken in ourselves. From a young age, we learned to ignore, control, deny, and reject our emotions. Few of us were given permission to actually *feel* our feelings. Unfortunately, when we stuff our feelings instead of finding healthy ways to express them, they leak out in other ways—ulcers, aggression, depression, and addiction.

I find the metaphor of a can of soda to be helpful. When we start believing that feelings are meant to be felt, we allow the emotions to bubble up to the surface instead of keeping them bottled up. They flow through us and dissipate when given the freedom to "pop" naturally. When we keep a tight lid on our emotions and prevent this from happening, every jostle of the can creates more bubbles, more pressure, and a greater explosive effect once that can is inevitably opened.

Accepting and expressing our emotions does not mean that we allow our emotions to control us. We don't allow the emotion to take over and don't excuse its unhealthy expressions. In fact, giving attention to a feeling actually keeps it from unconsciously driving us. Dr. Daniel Siegel and Dr. Tina Payne Bryson call this emotional regulation strategy "Name it to Tame it."[23] Identifying the emotion we're feeling actually calms our "emotional brain" and allows our "thinking brain" to evaluate the beliefs behind those emotions and make sense of our experience. We can name it, allow it, and then release it once it has run its course.

Feelings also come and go; they don't last forever. Understanding this can be helpful in giving ourselves permission to feel whatever we feel. We don't need to suppress unpleasant emotions or constantly chase the high of fleeting good feelings. We can make space for whatever emotions arise, knowing that they aren't final or absolute. *This too shall pass.* Let it simply wash over you.

No Good or Bad Emotions

Many of us were taught that big emotions are not acceptable. As children, when we were angry, we were punished; when we were upset, we were ignored. Our feelings weren't recognized or validated. They were curbed and denied. When our own children then go on and express strong emotions through meltdowns and tears, it's easy to get upset. They are showing feelings that we were never allowed to feel.

To rewire our understanding of emotions, we have to stop placing value judgments on them. When we label feelings as good or bad, positive or negative, we are tempted to manufacture the positive emotions and suppress the negative ones. We try to think only good thoughts, give off only good vibes, and stay optimistic. When we inevitably hit a bump in the road, we spiral into shame for feeling down or for having a hard time. We try harder to suppress the bad feelings, and in doing so we cut off parts of ourselves. We put on a face and play a part. We are our own puppet masters, but the strings are sadly not connected to our hearts.

This is not what wholeheartedness looks like. This is not how vulnerable authenticity shows up. Relentless positivity actually stunts our emotional health. We become scared of being scared, upset about being upset, angry for becoming angry. We are afraid of our own emotions.

Emotions are not good or bad—they just are. They are primal gut-level reactions. They are clues to what we believe and how we interpret our experiences. They are our teachers and messengers. By welcoming them and paying attention to them, we grow to understand ourselves, our needs, and our beliefs better.

As someone who often sees everything through a critical lens, my default emotions are usually anger or shame. I'm either upset with how the world is not as it should be, or upset with myself for not being as I should be. Untigering has taught me not to view these emotions as just another should or shouldn't. The reality is that I *do* feel them, so what can they teach me? How can I channel my anger for good and speak compassionately to myself when I feel ashamed or insecure? I've found that the more I learn to accept and welcome all my emotions, the more I'm able to do the same for my kids when they feel upset that their bubble milk tea spilled in the car or nervous about being the new kid at church.

ALL feelings are valid. All of them have some insight to share with us if we choose to listen to them instead of shoving them down. Our emotions provide us with a wealth of intuitive knowledge built into our bodies and brains, if only we learn to accept them without judgment. Providing ourselves with a safe space for our emotions allows us to connect with our own feelings and make room for our children's.

No Male or Female Emotions

My kids loved Perler beads when they were younger. Anyone who has worked with those little plastic beads knows that there are a hundred different ways for things to go sideways: accidentally knocking the peg board and sending the beads flying; over-ironing so the wax paper sticks to it; not ironing long enough for the beads to melt and the whole thing falling apart. It's pretty much a nightmare for any parent who is a control freak like me.

One time, Caleb had spent a good part of an hour meticulously working on a Perler bead rocket ship. He had been practicing ironing his bead creations with some success, but unfortunately, this time, it all crumbled to pieces.

"Oh no!" I exclaimed as I thought about all his hard work gone to waste. "Are you sad?"

"No," he said, fighting back tears. I went over to hug him.

"I would've been disappointed if that had happened to me," I told him.

Hearing that validation must have given him permission to be upset because his eyes immediately welled up as he buried his head in my lap. I held him close and let him cry. Later, I asked him why he had pretended to be fine when he was really upset.

"I thought you'd think that it was such a small thing to be sad about," he admitted. Somehow he had absorbed the message that some emotions were not safe to show.

Emotions are often seen through gendered lenses. It is culturally acceptable for boys to feel anger, confidence, pride, and drive, but not as safe from them to express sadness, fear, neediness, or sensitivity. They are conditioned by messages to "be a man," "toughen up," "grow some balls." This toxic masculinity denies them the freedom to express the full spectrum of emotions. The emotions that are suppressed and forced underground inevitably push their way to the surface through violence, depression, misogyny, etc.

Likewise, girls are taught that their emotions shouldn't be too "masculine." They shouldn't be too aggressive, too passionate, too forward. They should stay soft and sweet. When they do express big emotions, they're dismissed as "hysterical" or "hormonal." In China, it's expected for boys to be headstrong, gregarious, and impulsive ("Boys will be boys!"), but when girls behave the same way it's seldom interpreted quite as magnanimously.

The truth is that emotions don't have a gender. They are simply *human*. They are available and accessible to all of us. Seeing emotions in this way allows us to accept our children's feelings without trying to conform them to societal gender expectations about emotional expression. It is a non-binary, inclusive view that gives children freedom to feel all their emotions, whatever their gender.

Helping our Children Develop Emotional Intelligence

As parents, we can help our children accept and process their emotions, but we first have to learn how to do that with our own. We must create a safe space for emotions to be felt and expressed in healthy ways, modeling for our children through our own self-awareness. By describing our own feelings of frustration, inadequacy, excitement, gratitude, etc. we begin to give our kids the vocabulary to define their own emotions and the freedom to feel them. Emotions don't have to be scary, and they don't have to last forever.

We can also proactively help our kids connect with their own emotions. We may not have come from families that showed much emotional awareness or attunement, but we can still learn to reflect and empathize with our child's emotions. If they are still young and lack the language, we can help them identify and acknowledge the feeling: *"You're feeling upset because we couldn't get ice cream today. You're disappointed right now."* We can make a cautious observation: *"I saw that Jack took the toy out of your hand and you didn't want to play with him anymore. You probably feel scared that he'll do that again, huh?"* We can gently inquire: *"Is there something wrong? You seem upset about something."* The exact words aren't as important as the intention to express genuine empathy, which includes tone of voice and body language. The more we practice, the more we will have discernment to know how to connect with our child in a way that makes them feel loved, understood, and validated.[24]

It's important to withhold judgment and binary labels about our children's emotions, as well as acknowledge our own potentially biased interpretations. We should always recognize that our child knows their own emotions best. We are there to offer the language and help make connections, but not to impose our own perspective.

Only after experiencing our empathy is our child ready for the problem-solving stage discussed in the "Rethinking Correction" chapter.

CHAPTER 10

RETHINKING CONSISTENCY

We're often told that kids need consistency from parents. *Provide routine. Follow through on consequences. Stick to the rules. Be predictable.*

But my kids made me question this commonly held belief a few years ago. They had just written *The Secret Command*, a 19-page Minecraft saga, and wanted my feedback. I tried unsuccessfully to recommend Dad for the job, but finally agreed to give it a read-through. As a former English major with no interest in Minecraft or patience for grammatical errors, this was, quite frankly, TORTURE. It took all my focus and willpower to follow the dizzying plot twists and interpret the never-ending fight sequences but at the very end of the story something did catch my interest: the mother made an appearance. I decided to pay closer attention, knowing that the portrayal of this fictional mom was most likely inspired by one person: ME.

Suddenly, their mom came in and saw the zyrogorphmichypno-switcholeekysuper juice, all spilled on the floor!

"Clean this up, NOW! And all your LEGOS!" shouted James' and Hannah's mom.

I cringed. Is that how I sound to them? Do I only show up in their lives to nag them and yell at them? I read on, hoping that this mother would somehow redeem herself.

"Sorry, Mom. Our friends are waiting outside for us to play with them. We will clean up later," James said.

This was true, their friends were outside. James and Hannah walked out of the room, leaving their mom in the room.

She was actually kind enough to clean up the juice AND James' Legos when James and Hannah were playing with their friends.

They were home.

Huh... that was not where I saw the story going. But I liked it.

The mom changed her mind. She reassessed the situation and adjusted her course of action. She cleaned the room even though the kids had done nothing to deserve this favor. And ultimately, her kids didn't think of her as weak and wishy-washy, but as kind.

Steel vs. Bamboo

As untigering parents, we're often afraid that if we give our kids an inch, they'll take a mile. Every single grain of rice in their bowl must be eaten up, every toy in its proper place, every "i" dotted and "t" crossed. We believe this is comforting to our kids, knowing that their parent will always be steady and unchanging. We mean what we say and we say what we mean. Rarely will we make an exception or change direction mid-course. We are solid and dependable: like steel.

Unfortunately, the Titanic was also made of steel, and we all know what happened there.

So much faith have we in our own viewpoints that we often fail to recognize our weaknesses or the validity of another perspective. So stubbornly unyielding can we be that we plow ahead without considering the circumstances or being open to new information. We are so strict with our rules that our consistency becomes rigidity. But what happens to something hard and rigid when it meets with a blow?

It breaks easily.

The very strictness that we think makes us strong actually makes us brittle. Strength that doesn't know how to yield and compromise is susceptible to fracturing and cracking. Respect is damaged, joy is shattered, and communication breaks down when we rely on rules, formulas, and routines instead of relationship.

Instead of steel, we can strive to be more like bamboo—firm yet flexible... like the scaffolding outside a Hong Kong skyscraper.

"[The Western] concept of strength is, it doesn't move, it doesn't break. The Chinese concept is, you've got to bend with things. If you don't bend, you break. Bamboo's strength is in its ability to bend, and that's the miracle," says Dan Smith in a Newsweek article[25] about the wonders of bamboo.

Ping Fu, Chinese American entrepreneur and author of *Bend, Not Break*,[26] describes bamboo as being "flexible, bending with the wind but never breaking, capable of adapting to any circumstance. It suggests resilience, meaning that we have the ability to bounce back even from the most difficult times."

If we don't bend, we break. If we aren't flexible and capable of adapting to the circumstances, we snap and fracture instead of bouncing back.

Learning the art of bending requires us to be open to collaboration and negotiation. Instead of "my way or the highway," we are willing to hear input from our children. We choose to share power with them because we value and honor their perspective. We may not always be able to accommodate them, but when possible, we can look for win-win solutions that meet everyone's needs.

Becoming like bamboo means that we consider the circumstances and the child. It's easy to operate on autopilot and just rely on the rules and controls set in place, but flexibility requires us to attune to our child and adapt to the situation; to bend with the wind instead of trying to fight against it. It might not hurt to stay that extra thirty minutes to let your daughter play longer with her friends. Usually, you send your son off to bed on his own, but he's sick and feeling anxious—he may need your presence and comfort to fall asleep. Instead of letting our schedules and routines govern us, we can adjust to the child and the situation as necessary.

Yes, And

"Yes, and"[27] is a basic principle of improvisational comedy where participants are encouraged to accept whatever has been stated (yes) and then build on it (and). If a person rejects an idea in the middle of the scene, the whole act stalls and falls apart. But when participants are willing to roll with it, there's the opportunity to collaborate and create something interesting together.

The same is true of parenting. Saying simply "no" shuts down conversation and cooperation. It doesn't allow room for us to pivot, be spontaneous, or go with the flow. But the "yes" teaches us to listen carefully to our child so that we can respond appropriately. It interrupts our need to be in control. It creates a safe place for our kids to express their feelings, share their ideas, and make suggestions without fear that they will be automatically ignored or turned down.

The "and" allows us to adapt to the new information and create dialogue. It invites us into playfulness and partnership. I saw this "yes, and" approach dramatically play out one time when my kids were having an outdoor art class at a friend's home. At the end of the painting lesson, one of the kids—a particularly energetic boy—began rubbing his hands in the waterproof paint and splattering it around. I kept waiting for the mother to get her child "under control," but what she did instead totally shocked me. *She started playing with him.* She grabbed some paint on the paper plate palette and flung it back at him. She chased him around the yard, both of them laughing and screaming in delight, trying to tag each other with their dirty hands. After they had both worn themselves out, she brought him into the house and showered him off. What could have easily been a matter of punishment and control, she turned into a moment of connection and joy.

But "yes, and" doesn't mean we need to give in and agree unequivocally to whatever our kids want to do. It can mean we expand on the idea to make it work better. When your child wants to take a spontaneous trip to the beach, we can say, "That sounds so fun! And wouldn't it be nice if Daddy could come with us? Can we wait until next week so he can get off work and we can all go together?"

Sometimes, it's just about imaginative play and validation of feelings.

Child: *I really want to play with Sam!*

Parent: *I know. Who else do you miss visiting?*

Child: *Ari and Luis. I miss Corinne too.*

Parent: *What would you do if you could all get together for a play date?*

Child: *We'd swim in the pool all day and order pizza for dinner! Then they'd stay over for a sleepover and we could spend all night playing Sardines in the dark.*

Parent: *That would be really fun. We may not be able to do all that today, but maybe we can order some pizza.*

"Yes, and" can be a powerful antidote to our rigidity and inflexibility.

Yes, If

"Yes, if"[28] is the attitude that anything is possible if we approach the challenge with creativity and imagination. Rather than focusing on all the reasons why an idea won't work, we are inspired to think of ways to *make* it work. The orientation is always towards Yes rather than defaulting to No; we just need to find the right solutions and meet certain conditions. It empowers us to communicate our own boundaries and standards. It invites the child to collaboratively brainstorm and participate in the solution. "Yes, if" is a way to acknowledge their desires as well as our own so that we problem-solve to get everyone's needs met.

When our child wants to stay up late to watch a movie together, we can say, "Sure, if we can finish dinner and get cleaned up before 7:30. I have an early morning so I want to get to bed at a decent hour." The child gets to watch the movie and the parents will probably get willing helpers to clear the dishes and wipe the table, as well as a good night's rest. It's a win-win for everyone.

Yes, When

Sometimes, when we are unable or unwilling to agree to our child's desires or suggestions, instead of saying "no," we can have a "yes, when" mindset. This reframes a refusal into a delayed "Yes." Maybe the circumstances do not allow for it. Maybe it's not developmentally appropriate or safe as is. The focus is on the suitability of the situation and timing rather on the validity of the idea itself. It also shows that the rules aren't set in stone, and that we are open to accommodating them.

When our teenager wants to get a tattoo, we can say, "Why don't you do some research on all the pros and cons and we can talk about it some more?" It's not a hard and fast denial. It's an invitation to patience and negotiation as we build trust with one another.

Flexibility that is rooted in love and respect helps build resilient families in ways that consistency cannot. Sometimes, I'm a better parent when I'm *not* consistent—when I don't follow through on the consequence that I decided on in a moment of anger; when I flout the rules that I made thoughtlessly; when I'm like bamboo instead of like steel.

I may have inspired the mom in Noah and Caleb's Minecraft story, but the truth is, she has inspired me too.

CHAPTER 11

RETHINKING SUCCESS

We all want our children to lead successful, fulfilling lives. Yet it's important to consider what that actually means. How do we define success?

Traditional Definitions of Success

According to Amy Chua—the original tiger mother—success is about excellence and affirmation achieved through parental management:

> What Chinese parents understand is that nothing is fun until you're good at it. To get good at anything you have to work and children on their own never want to work, which is why it is crucial to override their preferences. This often requires fortitude on the part of the parents because the child will resist; things are always hardest at the beginning, which is where Western parents tend to give up. But if done properly, the Chinese strategy produces a virtuous circle. Tenacious practice, practice, practice, is crucial for excellence; rote repetition is underrated in America.

Once a child starts to excel at something—whether it's math, piano, pitching, or ballet—he or she gets praise, admiration, and satisfaction. This builds confidence and makes the once not-fun activity fun. This in turn makes it easier for the parent to get the child to work even more.[29]

In the eyes of Chua and other tiger parents, a child's personal preference, intrinsic motivation, and impulse to "follow their bliss" have no place in the pursuit of success. Instead, success is confined and defined by 3 S's:

1. **Status** – Recognition, praise, admiration, what others think. Our child's worth is based on where they stand in comparison with others. It's about position, prestige, and upward mobility. Pursuits that do not gain them status are frowned upon.

2. **Stats** – Their GPA, SAT score, or the ranking of the prestigious university they attend. Their trophies, awards, and championship wins. As they get older, it's their impressive salary, fancy titles, or the postal code of the upscale neighborhood they live in. These are the outward markers of achievement, the numbers and rankings and measurements that tell them whether or not they've made it.

3. **Status quo** – Children are expected to do what is practical and what will get them ahead in life. They are not encouraged to pursue their (pipe) dreams or take unnecessary risks. Instead, they are urged to stay in their lane and follow the tried and true paths that have worked for others.

Many of us grew up with these 3 S's, and while we may have gained a measure of success, we also found it stifling. We were placed on the hamster wheel of achievement to earn approval, and then we had to keep running in order to maintain it. It was more like a vicious cycle than a "virtuous circle."

How did we get here?

Factors that Shape our Views on Success

The ways we think about success weren't conceived in a vacuum. We internalized these values through our social conditioning, cultural context, and personal experiences. Let's unpack how some of these factors shaped our views.

Immigration

Whether documented or undocumented, for those of us who are immigrants or children of immigrants, there is often an unspoken pressure to prove ourselves and our worth. We need to show that we are upstanding citizens and contributing members of society so we're not branded as lazy freeloaders. We're expected to keep our heads down, know our place, work hard, and earn our right to be here. Furthermore, when our immigrant parents have given up so much, we feel like we have to make them proud and achieve a certain level of success in order for their sacrifice to have been worth it.

Immigrants also face untold obstacles that may limit their opportunities to achieve success, like language barriers, cultural differences, lack of accessible resources, and degrees and qualifications earned in their home country not being recognized in the States, just to name a few. Perhaps there were only certain fields and niches that opened the door for immigration or provided a livelihood. Whether the nail salon, the donut shop, the farm field, or the graduate school, these experiences influence our beliefs about the kind of success that is available to us.

Parents' education

As I mentioned earlier in the book, my mother was forced to quit school to work and support her family. Being a young girl, her education was deemed less important than her brothers', but that didn't stifle her love of learning. She was so determined to continue with her education that she found a way to keep up with her studies even while working. She was a bright student, eventually leaving her native Vietnam to study in Hong Kong where she went on to graduate at the top of her class.

For many of our parents, education is not something to be taken for granted. It is a hard-won privilege, the key to opportunity and upward mobility. They may overvalue formal education and be bewildered if we don't want to pursue it, seeing it as a necessity for success. Especially if they are highly educated themselves, a bachelor's degree is the absolute bare minimum for their children.

In contrast, parents who have learned to survive without a college degree may undervalue higher education and academics. They may be more focused on the daily grind of making money and think that studying Sociology or English Literature is a complete waste of time.

Our parents' lack of schooling, pursuit of schooling, or regrets about schooling shape how they communicate success to us and whether higher education is a necessary piece of the puzzle.

Poverty

Poverty has huge negative impacts on our life outcomes, often creating stressful home environments and affecting self-esteem as those who are disenfranchised compare themselves with those who seem to have "made it." The lack of opportunities and resources shape how we see ourselves and our ability to achieve success.

Furthermore, if we or our parents grew up impoverished, material wealth may be an important element of success for us.

We may desire the stability, status, and safety that money affords. We may wish for all the things that we were deprived of in our childhood.

Capitalism

The capitalistic mindset sees people as commodities, judging us on our worth based on our productivity. We are not intrinsically worthy; we are only valuable because of the profits we can bring in. Traditionally, this has fueled all kinds of oppression—from enslavement to child labor—as those with power exploit the vulnerable. Akilah S. Richards, unschooler and podcast host of *Fare of the Free Child*, had this to say about Black families: "For so many in Black culture, the way that we identify success and validation is through how much we produce or perform, and that goes back to enslavement, [when] our safety relied on how much we produced... There is a genetic and social imprint."[30]

This drive to produce and perform has been conditioned into us; we associate success with toil and a relentless ambition to achieve and impress. Rest, play, and contentment are antithetical to this definition of success.

Lack of representation

When we don't see people who look like us represented in certain professions, it makes it hard to believe those careers are within the realm of possibility for us. Fields like professional sports, music, film and TV, and the arts have so few Asian Americans represented. We're often discouraged from pursuing these interests before we even really start; we doubt we would ever make it past the gatekeepers.

Conversely, over-representation in certain fields can condition us to presume that those paths are the only ways to succeed. Indian Americans kids train for the National Spelling Bee, Filipinx Americans go into nursing, and Black students pursue athletic scholarships. While these are stereotypes, there is nothing wrong with them except when we mindlessly follow these tracks just because others have.

Family obligations

Many immigrants have family to support back in the home country, or extended family around who are relying on them. When my parents first came to the States, they sent all their earnings back to my grandparents who then gave them a small stipend to live on. This was not uncommon for that generation, and I'm sure it influenced the kind of success my parents pursued. When you have more than just yourself to think about, you can't be reckless and risky with what you do with your life. You have to consider your responsibility and choose your path wisely. You have to consider wealth in intergenerational terms. To do otherwise is selfish.

These are just a few of the factors that influence our definitions of success. While these experiences are nothing to be ashamed of, it's important for us to consider how we came to our beliefs about success so that we're not subconsciously controlled by them. Instead of just mindlessly continuing with our workaholic drive, overachieving tendencies, or limiting beliefs about ourselves, we can dig deeper to what is at the root of our behavior; we can deconstruct these definitions and motivations and evaluate them so that we can move forward with more intention.

As an untigering parent, you're probably finding that the traditional ideas of success have not served you well. Maybe you hit all those benchmarks of accomplishment but ultimately found them dissatisfying. You realize that much of what you did was driven by others' expectations rather than what was true about yourself. It's time that we redefine what it means to be successful so we can offer something more life-giving and liberating for our children.

Redefining Success

As is often the case for those of us who are deconstructing, I knew the kind of success that I wanted my kids to avoid, but it took a while before I found a definition that I really resonated with. I found it when I read this quote by Maya Angelou:

"Success is liking yourself, liking what you do, and liking how you do it."[31]

In other words, redefining success means that we empower our children to **define it for themselves**. However good our intentions or wise our perceptions, it's not our place to impose our own ideas of success onto our children. They must discover what it means for themselves as they explore who they want to be, what they like to do, and how they like to do it.

Liking Themselves

We want our children to have self-confidence and healthy self-esteem, but there are ways that we create obstacles to this through our parenting. One way we do this is by focusing on outward achievement. Whether we mean to or not, this makes our love feel conditional because our approval is dependent on what they do instead of who they are. Rather than communicating unconditional love and regard, our attention on their performance says to them, "You are only valuable if you _____." They are not free to just be. How else can they respond except with deep insecurity, anxiety, and perfectionism? We have taught them that they are not good enough. We have trained them to not like themselves as they are. Our kids may turn out to be high achieving athletes, musicians, entrepreneurs, and experts, but how much of their drive for success is driven by the desire to be good enough and worthy of love?

If we are constantly suggesting to our children that they need to succeed in order to please us, we are forcing them to hide away their authentic selves. They feel they must perform and perfect themselves in order to gain our approval. They can't show us their weaknesses, their failures, their quirks, their passions. Any love that we do show them feels disingenuous because we are just loving the false version they present to the world. They doubt we would accept them if they showed us what was behind the persona; indeed, we have given them little evidence that we would.

In order for our children to truly like themselves, Dr. Eileen Kennedy-Moore, in her book, *Kid Confidence: Help Your Child Make Friends, Build Resilience, and Develop Real Self-Esteem*, suggests three fundamental needs that must be met: **connection**, **competence**, and **choice**.[32]

Connection is a sense of belonging and meaningful relationships with others and is the foundation for a healthy self-concept. As parents, we are that first intimate connection in our child's life. We have tremendous power and influence to shape our child's sense of self. *Our children learn how to see themselves through our eyes.* We can drive them to achieve, making them believe that they are not accepted as they are; we can be disappointed in them when they fall short, causing shame and anxiety; or we can delight in them, reflecting back their worth and beauty apart from anything they do. Instead of overemphasizing behavior and performance, we can focus on creating an environment of unconditional acceptance. While a parent-child connection is crucial, extended family, friends, and communities where they feel a sense of belonging are also needed. This chorus of loving connections can help combat all the critical and judgmental messages out there.

Another fundamental need our children have is the need for **competence**. Untigering parents often feel good about this area— we sign them up for classes, find them tutors or coaches, help them gain skills and feel effective. Unfortunately, we also thwart our efforts through either our impossibly high expectations or our low estimation of their capabilities. While our high expectations and critical comments may be meant to help them improve, it really just makes our kids feel like nothing they do is ever good enough, fostering frustration and fear of failure rather than competency. And hovering over and rescuing them from difficulty instead of trusting that they can figure it out robs them of the ability to develop proficiency; it makes them feel incompetent. We can avoid these pitfalls by stepping back, managing our expectations, avoiding evaluation, and focusing on the process rather than the results. We can also break things down into manageable steps to set our kids up for success and encourage them to push through the challenges.

I'll admit, I'm not great at this. I can be very demanding and exacting and not the most patient of teachers. My kids help me with dinner once a week and it often devolves into one of them walking away in frustration because of my yelling or me just taking over because I want things done my way. I'm either an exasperated control freak who micromanages their every move or I'm so annoyed I leave them to figure things out on their own. Neither feels like a great way to help them build confidence or competence. I'm realizing that if I hope to instill in them a strong sense of their own abilities, I need to take my own advice and learn how to support and encourage them rather than make them feel inept.

The final need that Kennedy-Moore puts forth is a child's need for **choice**, which she describes as the ability to "make decisions, figure out what matters, and choose to act in ways that are consistent with personal values." Our kids need to be able to express their personal power and feel a sense of significance. This cannot happen when we rob them of self-determination. Sadly, too often their lives are tightly scheduled and closely monitored, whether at school or at home. There is no room for self-expression. They end up feeling helpless and frustrated instead of confident and resilient. If we want our kids to have a healthy self-concept, they need the autonomy to do significant things and make significant decisions. They need the freedom to express and experience their life in a way that emanates from the inside-out instead of molded from the outside-in, in a way that resonates with their own personal values.

While we cannot control how our children feel about themselves, there is much we can to do create an environment where their self-esteem will flourish. As we throw off the outer accoutrements of success and offer unconditional love, encouragement, and autonomy, our children can grow up knowing that they are worthy, capable, and loved as they are.

Liking What They Do

As mentioned above, a sense of personal power and autonomy is foundational for true success. If our children are to feel successful, empowered, and competent, it has to be on their own terms. That means giving them space to pursue and self-direct their own learning objectives, interests, and activities. That means giving up our compulsion to conform them to our own desires and definitions of success. For my family, that means we *unschool*.

If we think back to our own childhoods, how many of us took advanced classes, participated in extracurricular activities, or went into a field simply to pad our college application or please someone else? Did we actually like what we did, or were we just doing it to gain approval? Would we choose to do it again without any extrinsic motivation?

My partner, Jason, studied to become an electrical engineer, not for any great love of microchips but because he got into a good program at a good university and his parents pressured him to go. It was a respectable and stable career (not to mention very well compensated). He worked in Silicon Valley for a number of years and paid his dues, but it wasn't until we moved to China to become English teachers that he discovered his love of teaching. Hanging out with the students, instilling a joy in language and learning, and telling the same funny anecdotes year after year felt much more satisfying to him than his office job. His is just one example of how doing things because of other people's expectations or definitions of success doesn't satisfy us in the long run.

If success means liking what they do, our children need the freedom to pursue what they like. They need the freedom to dabble, play, and explore. For one child, it may be spending much of their day outside kicking a ball around. Another may like to spend it tinkering with electronics in the garage. My kids love to play video games and draw. Whatever the case may be, there needs to be intrinsic motivation instead of extrinsic punishments or rewards. They should be free to live out their true unique selves and not forced into standardized molds.

That's why I don't believe in having kids take violin lessons, join sports teams, or attend language immersion programs without their **enthusiastic consent**. Consent applies to more than just sex and bodily autonomy. Just as children have the right to determine how they use their own bodies to show affection and intimacy, they also have the right to determine how they use their body, soul, mind, intellect, and spirit to engage with the world. Whatever they do, they should be motivated to do without us pushing and pulling them where they don't want to go. Otherwise, they are just doing it to people-please or avoid punishment and will lose steam the minute we stop incentivizing them.

Liking How They Do It

Liking how they do things means that our children aren't beholden to arbitrary standards or schedules. They can follow their own learning styles instead of just being book smart. They can go at their own pace instead of competing with others to be first to the finish line. They can honor their need for rest instead of feeling like they'll fall behind. They can align with their own values instead of being driven by social pressure. And they can even quit if it's not a good fit instead of persisting in a bad situation to their own detriment.

Not every child wants to be a starting point guard, concert pianist, or high school valedictorian. Not every child is ambitious or has boundless energy. Some may be more contemplative or sensitive and are turned off by competitive environments. Others are playful and want to pursue their interests simply for the joy of it, not for the accolades. As parents, it's our role to observe our child and listen to them so that we can honor their personality and personal goals.

We see nowadays that many kids are very driven and successful, but they often pay a heavy price to achieve that kind of success. They willingly sacrifice their physical health, mental health, relationships, and their own integrity to reach their goals. A member of our Untigering parent group told us a disturbing trend among students: her niece, a premed student in college, found that it was very common for students to hide the resources in the library so others couldn't access them! I was flabbergasted at the lengths students were willing to go in order to get ahead.

Unfortunately, these are not isolated incidents. There was the recent college admissions scandal in the States where rich celebrity parents like Lori Loughlin and Felicity Huffman falsified information, cheated on entrance exams, and bribed school officials to get their children into elite colleges.[33] Things are not so different in China, where cheating is rampant and parents are often co-conspirators. A Chinese friend once told me how she had coached her grown daughter to cheat on an important certification exam. She instructed her daughter on where to sit, how to peek at her neighbors' answer sheets, and how to avoid detection.

I was appalled, but not surprised. When all that matters are the results, the ends justify the means. When children and their parents feel like everything is riding on that test score, that admissions letter, or that championship award, they will go to any length to secure the desired outcome. Sadly, that often leads to anxiety, depression, and even suicide when the pressure becomes too great.

The Dalai Lama XIV said, *"Judge your success by what you had to give up in order to get it."*[34] Success that is worth having is achieved with integrity and authenticity. Our children should not have to compromise themselves or their values in order to achieve it. They shouldn't have to sacrifice themselves at the altar of success.

If we want our children to like how they do things, we have to lower the stakes and emphasize the process rather than the results. We have to let them know that there are many paths to success, and many ways to live a fulfilling life. Showing our unconditional love and support for them no matter what their achievements gives them the freedom to fail and learn and grow. Instead of the frenzied drive to succeed, we encourage them to offer their gifts to the world in a way that feels honest and true. Instead of idolizing the cutthroat nature of high achievers, we model the importance of service, humility, and cooperation.

For many years, I was the quintessential picture of tiger motherhood: a woman with her arms crossed and her brows knitted, standing over a forlorn child perched on a piano bench. My kids had initially shown enthusiasm about learning piano, but long after their initial interest had waned, I continued to force them to take lessons. Many slammed doors and pounded keys later, I finally realized that making them continue was disrespectful to them and damaging to our relationship. I told my boys that they could stop learning piano if they wanted, fully expecting them to take me up on my offer.

Lo and behold, when given the choice, they actually wanted to continue; they just wanted to negotiate the terms. Noah, my eldest, told me that he got overwhelmed when too much was expected of him, so he wanted to learn fewer songs each week. Caleb liked the challenge and got bored when the songs were too easy. Instead of sticking to my own or the teacher's expectations, we adjusted so that Caleb would have a longer lesson than Noah. Although he was 2 years younger, he would learn more songs and progress more quickly, but that didn't bother Noah; he felt no need to compare or outperform his younger brother. For each of them, it was about enjoying and developing at their own speed, whether that speed was *allegro* or *andante*. I had originally thought that they didn't like what they were doing, but it turned out they just didn't like how they were doing it.

As parents, we need to honor our child's process. Not all children are going to be on the same timetable, hitting those milestones right on schedule. Some take longer, some speed through, and some have no intention of going down that path at all.

Parenting with an anti-oppression lens means that we do not overstep our bounds and colonize our children's lives with our own dreams and definitions of success. We can provide support and be a sounding board for them, but our children have every right to determine for themselves what a beautiful, meaningful, and successful life looks like.

In fact, instead of hyper-focusing on their achievements, one of the best things we can offer our children is to pursue success for ourselves—to like ourselves, like what we do, and like how we do it. As we cultivate our own passions and curate our own life, the need to live vicariously through our children will slowly ebb away. Parents and children alike will be liberated to live fully into how they define success for themselves.

Liking ourselves, liking what we do, and liking how we do it—this is a kind of success that is expansive rather than limiting, freeing rather than burdensome, inclusive rather than exclusive. It's a definition that says there is no one definition. We each get to define and redefine what success looks like for ourselves.

There's no day like today to begin.

PART 3
RAISING OUR CUBS

Every family is different, every parent is different, and every child is different. That's why I've tried to avoid giving prescriptive formulas and scripts for what to say or do. Yet I know it's hard to have something to hang your hat on if you've never seen peaceful parenting modeled. In this section, I'll be talking about some practical tools and strategies that have worked for me—ways to build autonomy, connection, and competency without leaning on oppression and coercion.

CHAPTER 12

CHECKING OUR ADULTISM

A s a society, we are so conditioned to using power over children that we justify all sorts of abuse and dehumanization that we ourselves would never tolerate. We live in a world where adults often receive preferential treatment and prioritization while children face prejudice and silencing. Just think of all the spaces where children are not free to be children, whether that be restaurants, churches, schools, or even our own homes. John Bell, Director of Leadership Development with YouthBuild USA, defines this pervasive adultism as "behaviors and attitudes based on the assumption that adults are better than young people, and entitled to act upon young people without their agreement. This mistreatment is reinforced by social institutions, laws, customs, and attitudes."[35]

In order to disrupt our adultism, we have to be intentional about challenging our attitudes and treatment of young people. We can ask the following three questions to check ourselves.

Would I do this to another adult/my partner?

If my adult friend cried about an upsetting situation, would I tell them, "It's no big deal," or roll my eyes at their pain? If my partner didn't make the bed, would I take away TV privileges or send them to the corner to think about what they did wrong? No, we intuitively know that treating another adult like that is unacceptable, and yet we so easily employ such abusive practices on our young people. Asking ourselves this question helps us to examine beliefs that paint children as less than and deserving of inhumane treatment.

How would I feel if I were treated this way?

If I were having an emotional meltdown, would I want to be ignored and isolated? If I made a mistake, would getting hit, yelled at, or shamed help me learn the right lesson and feel supported? If we ourselves would not respond positively to punishment, manipulation, violence, or emotional abuse, what makes us think that our children will? Considering this question is not only a practice of empathizing with our children, but also empathizing with our own inner child.

I was spanked as a child. I cannot recall any of the reasons why I was spanked, only the fear, helplessness, bitterness, and sense of injustice I felt towards my father whenever he ordered me to hold out my hand for punishment. For some reason, I buried those feelings and never thought to question whether or not I would hit my own children. If it was effective enough in keeping me on the "straight and narrow," it would do the same for my kids.

I was wrong.

I saw how it introduced fear, aggression, insecurity, and antagonism into our relationship. I noticed how my kids would flinch when I raised my hand or cower when I stormed toward them. I was reminded of how scared and vulnerable I felt as a child when caught in the grip of an adult's anger. I wondered, "Why am I doing this to my children?"

Learning to step back into the shoes of our childhood selves and remember our humanity helps challenge the many ways we dehumanize children. Instead of perpetuating the internalized oppression that we experienced as young people, we can grieve what we endured and seek to break the cycle with our own children.

Is this coercive?

Am I using threats, punishments, fear, physical intimidation, etc. to compel my child to do what I want them to do? Does my child have choice in this matter? Young people are routinely forced to clean their plates, share their toys, give hugs, and say sorry. We justify our control of their behavior, their bodies, and their belongings, feeling it is our right and responsibility to do so. Yet I imagine we would chafe at the thought of being forced to kiss someone on the cheek or handing over our iPad just because someone asked nicely. Children deserve to be treated as full humans instead of being robbed of their autonomy and agency. Acting upon them without their consent, willing agreement, and trust is simply oppressive.

With so many other positive tools to teach and protect our children, coercion is rarely necessary. Of course, there may be times when we will need to step in and act upon our children in ways they may not appreciate in the moment, whether it's for their own safety or the safety of others. However, when we respect their choices and boundaries 90% of the time, when that 10% comes around, there's enough trust and connection in the relationship for them to know that we have their best interests at heart.

These questions are not meant to paralyze us. They're not meant to be a formulaic algorithm with clear-cut answers. Instead, they are invitations to pause, to check our knee-jerk adultist reactions to the young people in our lives, and to intentionally do the work of anti-oppression.

We may notice that we become defensive when we have our adult power and privilege called out. Our parental fragility and defensiveness (similar to white fragility[36]) are cues that we are feeling threatened, and while understandable, we have to examine how this response serves to maintain the status quo and keep us from untigering. Our inability to own up to how we dehumanize children only serves to uphold oppressive systems and dynamics.

It takes humility to admit that we've made mistakes, that we've wounded our children, that we need to change. Humility is not about shame or self-deprecation or pity parties. Humility is actually a posture of courage and confidence: it is the courage of vulnerability and confidence in our intrinsic worth. It teaches us to accept our whole selves—including our weaknesses and limitations—as worthy of love and compassion. When it comes to our parenting failures, our radical self-acceptance can help us feel less threatened and more secure so that we can quiet our ego, break the cycle, and take responsibility for our wrongs.

Related to humility is the willingness to change and grow. We often talk to our children about a growth mindset, but we also need to apply a growth mindset to our parenting and personal growth. We need to be open to input and feedback, whether from books, articles, our partners, or our children themselves. We need to reframe our failures and mistakes as opportunities for learning and improvement instead of sources of shame. We need to be willing to question everything, especially because conventional views about parenting and attitudes towards children are often based on oppression and domination. A teachable heart means we are willing to be challenged and to learn new ways of relating to our children that are based on love and justice.

The burden is not upon our children to change, but upon us as the parents. This is an inconvenient truth when I'd rather deflect blame and play the victim, but the reality is that I'm the adult. It's my responsibility to get free. My children aren't to blame for triggering me, pushing my buttons, or driving me up the wall. I have to actively work through those triggers, remove those buttons, and tear down the wall instead of expecting my children to change their behavior before I change mine.

CHAPTER 13

ACCEPTING RATHER THAN ASSESSING

It's you I like,
It's not the things you wear,
It's not the way you do your hair
But it's you I like
The way you are right now,
The way down deep inside you
Not the things that hide you,
Not your toys
They're just beside you.
But it's you I like
Every part of you.
Your skin, your eyes, your feelings
Whether old or new.
I hope that you'll remember
Even when you're feeling blue
That it's you I like,
It's you yourself
It's you.
It's you I like.
– Fred Rogers

The other night, as I was squeezing Noah's arm affectionately during our bedtime routine, I noticed how lean and wiry he was. Compared to his younger brother whose arms are still fleshy and hands still dimpled, I could wrap my hand around Noah's entire bicep. I was about to make a playful comment about how he was all skin and bones when I stopped short.

I thought of the times in my childhood when someone had made a passing remark about my body. I recalled the shame I experienced when someone made me aware of my inadequacies.

And I held my tongue.

As a child, I learned early on that everything about me was subject to evaluation—my body, my behavior, my abilities (or lack thereof).

"Let's pull up that flat nose bridge of yours!"
"Looks like you've gained some weight."
"Don't be so shy."
"哎呀, your Chinese is so bad!"

For a people who have a reputation for indirect communication, Chinese family members can be surprisingly blunt.

But it wasn't just my family. In school, church, friendships, and society at large, I realized that I was always under the watchful, critical, evaluative gaze of the other. It made me profoundly aware that I was not safe. I was being watched. Judged. Weighed on the scales... and found wanting.

It wasn't just the criticisms either. The praise and compliments were just as insidious.

"Double-eyelids! Look at those big eyes!"
"You're such a good girl for helping with the dishes... unlike your sister."
"Iris is a very bright student."
"Don't you look pretty with those braids in your hair!"

Although the words were different, the reality was the same. I was being scrutinized. Appraised. Weighed on the scales and found acceptable... for now. All I had to do to gain approval was maintain this image.

I'm sure we can all relate to how a casual comment made a deep impression upon our psyche as a child; how a simple evaluation robbed us of our joy, made us self-conscious, and planted self-doubt. Regardless of how innocently these judgments were made, they caused us to censor and censure ourselves. And yet we so easily do the same to our children, looking at our kids through eyes of assessment instead of acceptance.

As a parent, I want to eliminate this evaluation from my relationship with my children. I want to remove any messages I might be sending that make them believe their worth is tied to their appearance, their attitude, their achievements.

Instead, I want them to know that they are unconditionally valuable and worthy, just as they are.

"Nothing you do could make me love you less. Nothing you do could make me love you more."

We cannot necessarily protect our kids from the toxic scrutiny prevalent throughout society, especially in this age of social media. But we can refuse to participate in it within our homes. Particularly while children are young and still forming their sense of who they are, we can create a safe space in our families where they can freely discover themselves without fear of judgment.

Witness Rather Than Judge

Many of us untigering parents are hypercritical of our children (and ourselves). We judge who they are—expressing our disapproval of their wildness, stubbornness, flamboyance, shyness, or sensitivity. Maybe we ourselves were judged for the same traits when we were children. Other judgments are rooted in social pressure. Western society often values certain traits over others: extroversion, athleticism, assertiveness, etc. In China, other traits may be emphasized: a calm nature, academic learning, submission, etc. Regardless of what the cultural values are, we as parents often try to fit ourselves and our children into those norms instead of honoring our child's unique nature. In our efforts to protect them (and ourselves) from attracting negative attention, our judgments cause us to box them in and label them.

My boys are both pretty low-key, introverted kids, especially among people they don't know well. They hate talking with strangers, do not like to be in the spotlight, and spurn friendly chit-chat. A few years ago, we took a vacation to the beautiful island of Phu Quoc in Vietnam. We were at the beach happily playing in the sand when I noticed another family making their way out to the water. They had a boy around the same age, and when he saw the sand structure that Noah and Caleb were digging, he went over to them and tried to strike up a conversation in his limited English. He was probably hoping to be invited to join in the fun, but while Noah and Caleb politely answered his questions, they were not overly enthusiastic about this interloper.

Noticing that they were having trouble including him, I went over and told them, "Be friendly! I think he wants to play with you!" They responded with a half-hearted effort. I felt bad for the boy, and annoyed at my kids. *I'll show them how it's done*, I thought to myself, offering the boy a shovel. A half hour later, I had not only befriended young Thang, but had accepted his mother's request to take pictures of her on my phone and become Facebook friends (I may have overcompensated a bit).

I was disappointed in my boys at first, feeling like they had missed out on an opportunity to show kindness. But then I realized that I was being unfair. I was expecting them to be immediately out-going and sociable instead of letting them take their time to warm up to new people.

Part of the untigering process for me has been to become a student of my children. To hold space for them to grow into themselves. To observe them and allow them to unfold under a gaze that delights in them without judgment. Do I know what my child is like? Do I know what makes them tick? Do I honor and accept my child's nature and work with it instead of against it?

We also judge what our children do—we can't seem to resist the urge to point out all the plot holes in their comic, refrain from passive-aggressively mentioning the 15 pounds they've gained, or hold back on critiquing their less than stellar performance on the court, stage, or exam. While our goal may be to help them improve and achieve excellence, we often end up discouraging them instead.

Rather than judging our children, we can learn to be witnesses instead. Judgment is about assuming a posture of superiority and authority, focusing on behavior and results, pronouncing conclusions and verdicts. Witnessing is about taking on an attitude of curiosity and respect, focusing on the heart and the process, listening and observing with open-mindedness. Shifting our perspective from judgment to curious observation teaches us to see our children with eyes of wonder and discovery. We avoid labels and allow them to surprise us as they unfold into their wholeness. We watch, notice, listen, learn, and accept.

Inquire Rather Than Evaluate

This non-judgmental curiosity moves us away from evaluation and towards inquiry. We stop centering our own perspectives and help our kids to develop their own by asking them about *their* opinions, *their* thoughts, *their* preferences. "How did you feel about how robotics class went?" "Which painting do **you** like best?" "Are you happy with how your project turned out?" "Do **you** like your haircut?" In doing so, we support them in becoming experts of themselves, attuned to their own bodies and emotions. Unless they specifically request feedback, we hold back on sharing our views or valuations. Even then, we can affirm them while teaching them to honor their own opinions: "Wow! You used the colorful glitter for the unicorn's horn! What's *your* favorite thing about your drawing?"

Few of us were treated with this kind of dignity as children. In my own childhood and even into early adulthood, I was cut off from my own sense of self. So much of my life was strictly controlled—decisions made for me and personal preferences ignored. I didn't know who I was or what I liked because my thoughts, feelings, and opinions were rarely valued or validated. I had a hard time naming my favorite movie or choosing a place to eat. Instead, I thrived in situations where I was told exactly what to do and what the expectations were, meeting everyone's standards without thought to my own. I wasn't awakened to my own power; I didn't know what to do with freedom.

While some of this was obviously due to my personality, I believe much of my disconnection and detachment from my self developed because of how I was disempowered as a child. Whether it was in my home, school, church, or other authoritarian institutions, I was taught to suppress my needs and desires in order to comply with adult expectations. This kind of environment leads to a lack of self-awareness, especially in more compliant children who aim to please.

If we want to raise our children to know themselves and own their voice and power, we need to shift from evaluation to inquiry. Doing so empowers children to self-reflect, self-evaluate, and take responsibility for what they have control over. It keeps us from projecting our values upon our kids, putting the ball in their court. Our children become more in touch with their own emotions, motivations, and agency instead of conforming themselves to accommodate us and others. Far from making them more self-centered, this emotional intelligence lays the groundwork for attunement and empathy towards others.

Encourage Rather Than Praise

One would think that positive parenting would affirm the use of praise and rewards over criticism and punishment, but such strategies are really just two sides of the same coin. They are all value judgments that express conditional love and approval. Even though praise and positive motivation may seem to bolster a child's confidence and encourage good behavior in the short run, it ultimately makes them feel less secure and less inspired to do the right thing.

Alfie Kohn, renowned author and lecturer on education, parenting, and human behavior, explains his critiques of praise: (1) Praise manipulates the child, acting like a verbal reward to control their behavior and encourage compliance. (2) Praise creates praise junkies, making them dependent on outside affirmation to feel good about themselves. They begin to tie their self-worth to the opinions of others and look to us or others for approval, making them vulnerable to people-pleasing and peer pressure. (3) Praise steals a child's pleasure, undermining their intrinsic motivation and joy and putting the focus on a parent's assessment. (4) Praise causes the child to lose interest, conditioning them to require our attention and affirmation in order to continue engaging in an activity or behavior. Without some sort of praise or incentive, they are no longer committed to do what they were praised for. (5) Praise reduces a child's achievement, locking them into a fixed mindset where they're afraid to fail or take risks because they want to maintain our approval.[37]

Some psychologists suggest focusing praise on effort and process rather than ability.[38] Other parenting experts advise applauding the deed rather than the doer.[39] These fail to recognize the inherent problem with using praise to encourage good behavior—the conditional and manipulative nature of such extrinsic positive reinforcements. Kohn cautions against any praise that is tied to behavior[40], especially in the context of a parent-child relationship where there is a disparity in power and status. I am apt to agree with him. There are other ways to encourage our children without making them addicted to our approval.

Kohn suggests, "Just paying attention to what kids are doing and showing interest in their activities is a form of encouragement. In fact, it's more important than what we say immediately after kids do something marvelous. *When unconditional love and genuine enthusiasm are always present, "Good job!" isn't necessary; when they're absent, "Good job!" won't help.*"[41] Encouragement isn't about giving our kids confidence from the outside in. It's about inspiring them to see the power and the courage that is already within themselves. We can offer this through our consistent engagement and loving presence in their lives, our non-judgmental witness that communicates trust in our child's process and competence, and our curious inquiry that values their perspectives.

Offer Random Acts of Love

It's easy enough to give positive attention when our kids perform what is expected of them or present themselves in ways that please us, but when we unconsciously limit our affection and affirmation to those moments, it feels like our love is dependent on their behavior. Our acts of love and affection just become tools of power and manipulation.

If we want to communicate unconditional love to our children, we must do so in ways that are not contingent upon their obedience, performance, attitude, or anything other than their existence. Throughout the day, we can offer random acts of love and kindness—hugging them, smiling at them, and telling them we are proud of them, apart from anything they do. These affirmations communicate that we love them without conditions or strings attached.

Few of us have experienced this kind of unconditional love. We've never had this modeled to us; we don't know what this actually looks like. Especially for those of us who grew up in families where love, affection, and affirmation were rarely expressed (even when we did everything right!), expressing (and receiving) unconditional love feels foreign. How many of us became overachievers in order to seek our parents' approval? How many of us are still longing for their acceptance?

Yet despite our lack of experience, we can break the cycle and forge a new way for the next generation and those to come. I believe we all intuitively know how unconditional love should make us feel—empowered, free, safe, known, accepted—and I'm sure that is what we want for our children. When we show them unconditional positive regard no matter the circumstances, in the everyday moments of life, they learn to trust in themselves and in our love for them.

This may all sound idealistic and unrealistic. But as I mentioned at the beginning of the book, untigering is about embracing the growth and the process, not about getting it perfect. Is my love conditional? Yes! Do I sometimes judge, evaluate, and criticize my kids?

Absolutely. Am I tempted to manipulate my kids? For sure. But as I become more aware of the harmful consequences of this kind of parenting, it's incumbent upon me to change and learn healthier practices that help my children thrive.

As social creatures, our kids are naturally wired to look to others to help them gain a sense of who they are. What they see in our eyes matters. When Noah and Caleb look into my eyes, I hope they never wonder how they measure up, what they're worth, or where they stand. I hope they see reflected back to them this one truth:

"It's you I like."

CHAPTER 14

EACH CHILD IS AN INDIVIDUAL

In the previous chapter, I addressed our need to accept our children for who they are. In this chapter, I go into further detail about different aspects of our children's nature we can strive to accept unconditionally.

Temperament

When Noah was four, I brought him to a library event for kids. I thought it would be fun for him—an indoor trampoline, craft activities, organized songs and games. But while other kids were having a blast, he spent the entire time clinging to me or cowering in the corner, refusing to participate. I was frustrated—why should I go out of my way to bring him out when he didn't have the decency to enjoy himself?!

It took me many other similar missteps before I realized that I was totally missing his cues and misunderstanding his nature. I had assumed that he was like other rambunctious 4-year old boys who loved being loud and physical, who enjoyed the 热闹 (liveliness) of parties and people. But Noah was not like that. He needed time to warm up to new situations. He found new environments stressful and overwhelming. He disliked loud noises and large crowds. His sensitive nature was even revealed in his reactions to food and temperature: he had a delicate stomach, and his skin would often break out in welts when it was windy or cold.

Once I began to understand and accept him, I learned to parent him in a way that was more in harmony with who he was. I allowed for a lot of quiet down time for him to observe and explore. I didn't overdo it with social events. I avoided one-off activities that he wouldn't enjoy anyway. I minimized large gatherings with strangers and instead had regular playgroups in my home with a small group of kids and moms. I learned to follow his lead and celebrate his individuality. I'm still learning to this day.

As parents, we have to work through our own preconceived notions of who our children are or how they should behave, releasing those expectations so that they can be free to show up fully and authentically. Instead of making assumptions about them, we need to observe them and allow them to teach us about who they are.

Here are some factors to ponder as we seek to better understand our children's temperaments:

- Emotional intensity
- Activity level
- Frustration tolerance
- Reaction to new people
- Adaptability
- Need for routine
- Attention span
- Sensory threshold

Write down your observations about your child in these different areas. Avoid judgments or your own projections of what's right or wrong, good or bad. Instead, try to see with eyes of compassion and acceptance of your child's unique nature.

The world is in need of the rich diversity each individual offers—we need the go-getters and the hold-uppers, the doers and the philosophers, the feelers and the thinkers, the leaders and the supporters. Just like biodiversity is important to a thriving ecosystem, when we come together and celebrate our unique gifts, our communities become more robust and resilient. Embracing our child's essence thus helps create an environment where not only they flourish, but we all do as well.

This simple exercise may expose ways that we have failed to accept our child unconditionally. It may bring to light aspects of their nature (and our own) that we have not honored or understood. Feelings of shame and regret may rise up. It may trigger grief about the ways that we were not accepted as children. This is our opportunity to process our own pain, ask forgiveness of our child, and adjust our parenting to align with our child's temperament so that we break the cycle.

Interests

Tiger parents often see the outward markers of success and train their children to hit those targets: academic excellence, sports, debate, leadership, part-time jobs, community service, music, dance, art... pretty much anything that will look good on a college application. We don't ask whether or not the child is interested, gifted, or motivated to engage in these activities. The child's own personhood is completely irrelevant. What matters is that the child stays ahead of the game and maintains a competitive edge.

As untigering parents, we want to avoid this unhealthy grooming that violates a child's autonomy. In order to honor the individuality of each child, we need to learn to follow their lead instead of taking the lead. While we have the power to influence and shape our children's interests, we cannot assume that they will follow in our footsteps or insist that they participate in our hobbies.

On the flip side, we must be careful not to judge or discredit their interests simply because *we* find no value in them. We may not be entertained by Minecraft, Captain Underpants, or bottle flips, but that doesn't mean it holds no value for our kids. They are their own person. A fascination with guns or obsession with makeup does not mean that a child is sociopathic or superficial. They may just be exploring their sense of power through play, or expressing their creativity and artistry. We must not catastrophize and assume the worst of their motivations and passions, but give them room to explore while staying curious and connected. By empowering and resourcing our kids to pursue their own interests without judgment, we enter into their world and communicate unconditional support.

Love Language

Many of us are familiar with Dr. Gary Chapman's work regarding the five Love Languages.[42] It is built on the premise that each one of us gives and receives love in primarily one of five different ways:
- words of affirmation
- quality time

- gifts
- acts of service
- physical touch

Understanding which love language speaks most to our child helps us to meet their needs and communicate love in a way they can receive. Do they light up when we give them encouraging words? Do they crave one-on-one time with us? Do they enjoy receiving gifts as a symbol of our love? Do they really appreciate it when we help them in some way? Do they love cuddling, back rubs, tickles, or rough housing? You and/or your child can take a quiz at www.5lovelanguages.com/quizzes to discover what their love language might be.

Love languages are different from child to child. Just because one responds well to gifts doesn't mean that that's meaningful for the other. And just because we enjoy expressing and receiving love in a certain way doesn't mean that that is true for our child. Words of affirmation may feel empty to them if what they really want is quality time. All the things that we do for them as parents may go unappreciated if they'd much prefer an affectionate hug over a fancy meal. Attempting to express love in ways that don't match our child's love language means that something gets lost in translation. We may be expending a lot of energy and offering a lot of love, but the child doesn't feel loved. It's like pouring a pitcher of water but missing the cup entirely. If we want our child's cup to be filled, it's important to identify the unique way our child feels loved so that we can communicate our affection effectively.

Development[43]

We often have unrealistic and unfair standards for our children—ones that don't take into account the child's developmental stage. We want babies to stop crying and sleep through the night, toddlers to stop being so irrational and self-absorbed, and teens to stop experimenting and pushing back. Little do we know that these undesirable behaviors are actually developmentally appropriate. Babies are learning to trust, attach, and have their needs met when they cry and wake. Toddlers have little impulse control and are growing into their sense of self. Teens are discovering their own identities and independence.

When our kids are struggling, more often than not, they are either (1) not developmentally mature enough to do what we expect of them or (2) they require more training to gain the skills needed. Understanding a child's unique development, neurobiology, social-emotional growth, and emotional maturity at each stage can help us to adjust our expectations. We can begin viewing the triggering behavior as a cry for help rather than a scream of defiance. We can more readily offer the compassion and support they need instead of judging them too harshly.

There may be children who seem to be "easy," "good," and "obedient," no matter what developmental stage they are in. Some of it may be temperament, but in my own experience as a poster child for "good girls," much of it was at the expense of my own needs, emotions, and autonomy. I was trained to behave like an adult before I was an adult. People considered me mature for my age, but in many ways, I was simply not allowed to be a child. Honoring our child's individuality requires us to have developmentally appropriate expectations so that we don't unintentionally bulldoze over their needs.

Gender Norms and Sexuality

As we are growing in our understanding of human sexuality and gender identity, it is important for us parents to not make assumptions about how our children show up in the world or who they will be attracted to. Children are still developing their sense of self and we have to be careful not to box them into gender stereotypes that make them unsure of our absolute love for them. We need to pay attention to their cues instead of forcing gendered norms upon them.

As a young girl, I loved wearing frilly dresses, putting on lip gloss, and getting my long hair curled, despite the fact that it meant losing a night of sleep in uncomfortable plastic rollers. As I grew older, I played around with wearing oversized men's shirts and androgynous fashion; I even got a shaved haircut my senior year of high school. It was typical teenage experimentation and—despite my parents' side-eyes—I found that it was socially acceptable for me as a girl to blur these gender lines. Boys are usually not given the same freedom to engage in gender-bending expressions or traditionally feminine pursuits without significant social fallout.

When it came to raising my boys, I sadly didn't think twice about confining them to the gender binary, dressing them in "boy" clothes, with "boy" themes, in "boy" colors. I exposed them to books, toys, and media about sports, dinosaurs, and vehicles—things that I assumed they were interested in simply because they were boys. Then, I began to notice that Noah liked pushing around the baby doll in the toy stroller and would even sometimes pretend to breastfeed it. Caleb loved wearing sparkly jewelry and playing with the toy kitchen set. I realized that I needed to stop defining their gender expression for them and simply follow their lead.

Binary distinctions between masculine or feminine are capricious social constructs. They differ from culture to culture and age to age. K-pop boy bands like BTS openly wear makeup and celebrate a kind of masculinity that challenges traditional Western norms.[44] Blue used to be associated with baby girls.[45] Men were the first to wear high heels.[46] All this goes to show how subjective and fickle these rules are.

The problem lies not only in the shifting sands of gender norms, however. All gender stereotypes, even if they are consistent throughout history and culture, are harmful and limiting. When we label boys as being tough, strong, physical, and assertive, we shame them when they are vulnerable, sad, reserved, or cautious. When we typecast girls as being nurturing, sweet, passive, and demure, we criticize them for their anger, passion, leadership, and sexuality. Whatever the stereotypes are, they keep our children from freely expressing their whole selves, especially the parts that don't fit social expectations.

As our children grow and become more aware of their sexuality, we should avoid the presumption of heteronormativity. Seemingly innocent discussions about who they want to marry, how many children they want, which boy/girl they think is cute, etc. ignore the beautiful array of relationships and attraction. Instead of assuming they will end up in a heterosexual marriage with 2.5 kids, a dog, and a white picket fence, we can provide information and exposure to the spectrum of identities, families, and relationships, especially those that lack representation and understanding. By talking about a variety of sexualities, gender identities, and families in a non-judgment way, we make it safe for our children to embrace their own unique sexuality and share it with us, whatever it may be.

Nowadays, when Noah dances around with a ribbon wand or Caleb shows off his flip sequin shirt featuring sparkly cats with heart-shaped eyes, I can smile and delight in their freedom and joy and self-expression. When Noah expresses anxiety or Caleb needs a hug, I can hold them and hold space for their big emotions without expecting them to be tough. I hope that as they grow into their gender expression and sexuality, I can embrace them fully with love and acceptance, unburdened by fear or judgment.

―――――◈―――――

These are just a few of the areas to consider as we seek to honor the individuality of each of our children. Armed with new instincts and a greater understanding of our children, we can tailor our parenting to the individual needs of each child instead of relying on formulas and scripts. What expresses love and connection to one child may feel overbearing to another. What requires a soft response in one situation may require stronger boundaries in another. As we embrace the complexities of ourselves and our children, we avoid a one-size-fits-all approach and instead attune to our child, the situation, and our own intuition.

CHAPTER 15

BUILDING CONNECTION

Tiger parents are involved parents.

We ensure our children finish every grain of rice in their bowls, check that their homework is completed, and supervise the practice of their musical instrument of ~~torture~~ choice. We shuttle them to school, soccer practice, church activities, and Chinese school on the weekends. Unfortunately, our investment *into* our children too often fails to translate into connection *with* them.

Connection is the bond that develops when you are known and valued; a deep sense of being seen, safe, soothed, and secure.[47] Sadly, I'd venture to say that few of us grew up with this kind of strong emotional attachment to our parents. We might have felt love and appreciation for them, but connection? Likely not. When it comes to our own children, we lack models and examples of how to build connection beyond cooking food and providing for basic needs.

So what's an untigering parent to do?

In this chapter, I offer a few concrete ideas and practical tips to experiment with.

Special Time

There are many ways to build connection with your kids, but one powerful way is to simply spend some "special time" with them: intentional, individual time with your child doing whatever they want to do. Even something as little as 5-10 minutes every day develops a sense of belonging and love. It interrupts our tendency to herd them through the day from one to-do item to the next and slows everyone down so we can actually take time to enjoy each other.

The possibilities are endless!

- Reading a book
- Having a dance party
- Playing a game
- Debriefing the day before bedtime

There are no rules except to have one-on-one time doing something the child enjoys. But a word of caution: don't sabotage your efforts by forcing your own objectives on them, however beneficial or educational. Our kids can smell this from a mile away! Instead, let your Daddy Time or Mommy Time be an invitation, without any agenda except to connect.

I found this practice to be very helpful, especially when my kids were younger. I had a lot of repairing to do after years of tiger parenting, so having a daily special time with each of them was healing for our relationship. As they've gotten older and as our connection has deepened, their need for Special Time has changed. Nowadays, it looks more like impromptu family snuggles, heart-to-heart conversations in the car, or game nights together.

Show Affection

Many of us did not come from physically or emotionally affectionate families. We grew up marveling at all the bear hugs and kisses that were common among our white friends and in those picture-perfect family sitcoms. In contrast, there were maybe only a handful of times in our childhood when we received a gentle pat or an awkward hug from our parents.

Research[48] shows, however, that loving touch is essential for healthy thriving, not only in infancy but on into adulthood. It can lower blood pressure, boost immunity, and produce emotional well-being. If that is not enough to convince us, perhaps the fact that meaningful touch also improves brain functioning will induce us to be more physically affectionate with our kids. Hugging our children actually makes them smarter!

So offer your children a lot of physical affection; not just when they're infants, but even as they get older. Continue massaging, hugging, snuggling, and kissing them, if that's what they enjoy; yes, even—and perhaps, especially—our boys, who are often conditioned to reject touch and gentle affection. My tween boys sometimes still hold our hands, sit on our laps, and give us kisses on the lips. We've never shamed them into thinking that this was no longer appropriate for their age.

Be in tune with what kind of loving touches they enjoy, and how much. Don't tickle them when they've asked you to stop. Don't smother them with squeezes when they're ready to run off and play. Consent is key. (For more details, see the chapter "Bodily Autonomy".)

Talk Less

Tiger parents lecture way too much. We try to reason and explain and problem-solve too soon and too often. Our well-intentioned advice often ends up antagonizing and exasperating our kids. Not only that, but it is rarely effective. With all the conflicts that arise from our talking *at* children and giving talkings *to* children, perhaps we need to learn to just shut up and talk less. Instead, we can:

- *Become better listeners.* Invite our children to share their thoughts, opinions, and feelings. Empathize with them and validate what they say. Understand their perspective instead of imposing our own.
- *Become better observers.* Notice what piques their curiosity, makes them laugh, or sets them off. Pay attention to what unmet needs or stresses might be causing them to act out: over-tiredness, hunger, fear, etc.
- *Become better coaches.* Ask the right questions instead of always offering the right answer. Avoid solving their problems for them, but give them tools to handle it themselves.

My kids were roughhousing the other day when it got a little out of hand. Caleb came up to me to complain that Noah had hit him too hard. Instead of playing the referee, I decided to be a coach.

"Tell Noah about it," I said to Caleb, encouraging him to speak directly to his brother. I could have just intervened and reprimanded Noah, but I wanted Caleb to know that he could set his own boundaries and that I would support him in doing so.

Caleb turned to his brother. "I don't like being hit so hard. Stop doing it." Noah agreed to respect his boundaries and the conflict was quickly resolved.

Talking less shows that we honor our children's voice and have confidence in their abilities. There's no need to constantly assert our own perspective. Too many words without a foundation of connection will just be tuned out anyway. The next time we feel like sermonizing, let's bite our tongue and step down from the pulpit so we can listen, observe, and coach instead.

Smile More

My children are quite familiar with my furrowed brow and with-ering glare. Only for their most exceptional feats do they receive the rare gift of a smile. (This may also explain why Asian women are known for aging so well: infrequent smiling is our secret to preventing laugh lines and crow's feet.) This is, sadly, not just the case with my children. Back in college, Jason was giving a public talk one time when he looked out into the audience, searching for some moral support from me, his girlfriend. All it took was one look at my face and he decided to block me out, homing in on the encouraging smile of our friend, Angelia, instead. Some people just can't handle a good RBF.[49]

With our kids especially, sometimes we are so intent on molding them that we forget to actually enjoy them. Our eyes are so focused on their future that we fail to witness how precious they are in the present moment. I don't want my kids going through life knowing that I love them yet unsure if I actually *like* them. I want to take every opportunity to show them how much they delight me.

I just need to get my face on the same page.

If scowling also comes more naturally to you than smiling, here are some questions to ask yourself:

- What about my child brings me joy?
- Do my eyes light up when I see my child?
- Does my demeanor communicate delight? Or does it com-municate displeasure, frustration, and apathy?
- Do I make eye contact with them when they're talking to me?
- How can I take time to get my needs met so that I can be less grouchy?

Our children intuitively pick up on not just our spoken words but our unspoken communication as well. Becoming more aware of how our disposition and body language affect our kids can help us become more mindful. For me, I'm learning to unclench my jaw and soften my eyes, relax my eyebrows and turn up the corners of my mouth. While I'll never be an Angelia, I'm being intentional about cultivating delight and joy in my children. My face is learning to do the same.

Playfulness

Playfulness and spontaneity do not come naturally for me, especially in my parenting. When my kids were young, I'd go through the motions of peekaboo, This Little Piggy, and stacking blocks over and over again, but found it all absolutely mind-numbing. I found babbling pointless, imaginative play draining, and silliness... well, silly.

While play may not be natural for many of us, it is the natural language of learning and connection for our children. In his book *Playful Parenting*, Lawrence J. Cohen asserts that children use play to discover the world, develop confidence and mastery, connect and reconnect, and recover from emotional distress.[50] As parents, it's a powerful way to enter into their world, create joy and intimacy, and shift negative energy. It disrupts our desire for control, structure, and convenience so that we engage with our children as partners rather than task masters.

For me, playfulness is actually an intentional practice I pursue. It helps break through my hypercritical and perfectionistic impulses and challenges me to not take myself (or my kids) so seriously. It encourages me to rekindle that childlike exuberance and lightheartedness that we see so easily in young children.

The possibilities for playful parenting are endless: speaking in a silly voice when trying to get kids out the door, making household tasks into a game, turning on the music and dancing while cooking together, pillow fights to get out energy, reverse role playing in order to solve a problem, play-acting with stuffed animals to talk about our feelings, and, of course, actually playing games together.

The only limits are our imagination and our willingness to slow down and loosen up.

Building connection is unique for each parent and child. Use these as springboards for connection, not as formulas. The deeper your connection grows, the more intuitive you will become about how to make your child feel seen, safe, soothed, and secure.

CHAPTER 16

FAMILY MEETINGS

When I was a teenager, my parents decided to introduce weekly family meetings. Every Sunday evening, my preacher father would lead us in a time of Bible study, prayer, and singing hymns in three-part harmony, with perhaps a "fun" element thrown in, like a round of the Ungame or a couple hands of Big 2. My parents were no doubt making an effort to be more engaged with us, but all I remember is that I did not enjoy it. I resented the coercion, the pedanticism, and how contrived it all felt. Many years later, when I was comparing notes with Jason, I found out that he had very similar family meetings that consisted of Bible studies and long lectures. It must have something to do with religiously devout authoritarian fathers.

When I had kids of my own, I had no interest in family meetings, at least not the kind that I grew up with. My kids were also young and the thought of trying to do one with two toddlers was laughable. It wasn't until I was introduced to a different kind of family meeting—one that was rooted in connection, respect, and joy—that I started getting excited about the possibility.

Casper ter Kuile, author the *The Power of Ritual* and co-host of the *Harry Potter and the Sacred Text* podcast, has this to say about how to create community together: *"When you want people to feel like they belong to one another, to a place, to a bigger story, they have to feel like they're co-creating it, not just consuming it."*[51]

Co-creation, not simply consumption. Consent, not coercion. Despite my parents' good intentions, these were some core values that were missing in what it meant to be a family and have meaningful shared experiences together. We, as the children, had no power. We were not seen as having the authority or ability to give input or have opinions. We were considered passive actors who just needed to play the role that was given us.

Family meetings, when done with children as co-creators, can be a practice of empowerment and liberation, teaching young people that they have voice, responsibility, and agency in helping to create and shape family life. It honors the value of each member and celebrates whatever they can offer, no matter their age or ability. Parent and child alike feel invested in what they're building together and grow in their sense of belonging. When we set aside a regular, intentional time for this liberatory practice of co-creating, it can truly be a powerful ritual and source of bonding.

Here are some thoughts about how to get started with family meetings.

Give it a Fun Name

Very few of us get excited about the word "meeting"; children even less so. It can feel so stuffy and serious. So choose a name that elicits excitement and joy. We call ours *Table Talk Time*. Get your kids' input and see what fun and funny names you can come up with.

Set a Regular Time

Find a regular time where you're unlikely to have scheduling conflicts or other obligations. Then, try to stick to it so that it becomes a part of your family's rhythm. The frequency depends on the needs and preferences of your family, but since the purpose is to create a sense of belonging together, try not to go too long without checking in with each other. It doesn't have to be long and drawn out either; even 15 minutes can be sufficient. Our family chose Sunday evenings as a good time for us to look ahead and plan for the coming week. It has become a part of our weekly routine and something that we all look forward to.

Assign Roles

Unlike my childhood family meetings where my father was always the one in charge, we can find ways to empower our kids and give them agency. One way to do this is by having them be in charge of a certain aspect of the meeting.

For us, since we are a family of four, we decided on 4 different tasks that we would take turns being responsible for:

1. Leading – facilitating discussion
2. Snacks - choosing and preparing snacks
3. Calendar - going over our schedule for the coming week
4. Special Thing - choosing a fun thing to do together (game, movie, etc.)

Even young kids are able to do this with our support and coaching. We can offer input and guidance, but try to avoid vetoing or trumping their decisions. Even if they choose marshmallows and Cheetos for snack time, try to honor their choice. Even if they insist on playing base-ball out in the sweltering heat, try to go along with it. Doing so shows them that they do, in fact, have power, and you will, in fact, respect that power. This is a good practice in mutual compromise, and you can always remind yourself that you will get your turn to choose next time!

Have a Structure

It's helpful to have a loose structure and agenda so everyone knows what to expect week to week. For us, it has morphed over time, but this is generally what we do:

- *Appreciations* - We start by expressing appreciations and affirmations for each other, saying positive things we've noticed throughout the week. Taking the time to proactively appreciate each other keeps us focused on what the other person is doing right. For us, this has spilled over into daily life, as we now more readily thank each other for helping out or being kind.
- *Mistakes* - We introduced this when we noticed our kids struggling with failure. We wanted to normalize mistakes and see them as opportunities for growth, so now we have a time where we can share big and small mistakes to laugh about and learn from.
- *Things we're proud of/Hard things we've done* - This is an opportunity for us to share challenges we've overcome and celebrate our accomplishments. When we share how we're growing and learning, it helps to build confidence, self-motivation, and a growth mindset. It also keeps us in touch with each other's interests and projects so we can support and encourage one another.
- *Problem-solving* - During this time, we bring up any agenda items that have come up during the week. (Some fami-

lies post up a sheet of paper to write down problems or concerns beforehand.) We've found that waiting until our Table Talk Time to address different issues has been really helpful. When we bring it up in the heat of the moment, we can often be upset or distracted. Waiting until there's been some time and distance helps us to sift through what needs to be discussed and what can be overlooked. Rather than simply reacting to the situation, we're more calm, present, and able to think clearly.

Truthfully, it's usually Jason and I who bring up something: how to use the bathroom without getting pee everywhere, reminders of where the dishes go, etc. Sometimes we just need to take time to train... and train... and train. Jason loves to sleep in, and it probably took him at least 2 years of consistently training them on morning etiquette (how to open/close doors quietly, how to feed themselves breakfast, how to keep their voices down) before he was able to stop bringing it up as an agenda item.

Other times, we need to brainstorm solutions together. Asking them for solutions instead of lecturing them helps to encourage buy-in and cooperation. When we work together to deal with the problem without blaming or nagging, our kids often come up with creative answers.

If my kids don't bring up anything as an agenda item, sometimes I ask them, "Is there anything that I can be doing better?" It shouldn't just be a teachable moment for the kids, but also a safe place for kids to lovingly confront parents.

While problem-solving together is a powerful way to honor their voice and gain cooperation, don't overdo it! Trying to deal with 10 different issues in one meeting can end up being discouraging and overwhelming. Pick a few issues to work on and then table the rest for next time.

- *Calendar* - This is a time for us all to get on the same page about what is happening in the coming week. We write down relevant events on our large wall calendar: upcoming birthdays, outings, meetings, etc. This helps us to prepare and plan around each other. If I have an online meeting at 11:00 am, the kids know to be quiet and ready to get off the internet if there's not enough bandwidth. If we have a library run scheduled for Wednesday, they know to pack up their books and be ready to go. I may still need to remind them, but at least it's not coming out of nowhere.

  Having a family calendar also means I don't have to be the one responsible for everyone's schedule.

Kid:	*"What time is my Outschool class?"*
Me:	*"Look at the calendar."*
Kid:	*"What day are we going to Auntie Caris' house?"*
Me:	*"Look at the calendar."*
Jason:	*"When is the…"*
Me:	*"Calendar."*

- *Special Thing* - We take turns choosing the special activity to do together as a family. It doesn't have to be anything fancy or complicated, but it should be fun! Even if it's not our cup of tea, we encourage each other to go along with whatever is chosen. This not only teaches us to compromise and be flexible, but to consider each other as well. I've learned not to choose jigsaw puzzles because, while I enjoy them, the rest of my family, not so much. My boys have learned not to suggest video games because Jason and I are completely incompetent at them. Through trial and error, we've found things that are enjoyable for all of us. We've done movies, board games, dance parties, outdoor sports, walks to the corner store for some ice cream… Get creative with it!

My boys were only 2 and 4 years old when we started Table Talk Time and we are still going strong, eight years later. For your own family meeting, take what is helpful here and ignore the rest. Tailor it according to your family's interests, ages, and values. Whatever form it takes, root it in co-creation, respect, and playfulness.

CHAPTER 17

BODILY AUTONOMY

"**Y**ou're not the boss of me!"
While we may disdainfully imagine an impertinent tween yelling this at us, there's actually truth in this statement. The illusion of control over our children is just that—an illusion. The bubble is popped when our child decides to exert their own will by refusing to go to sleep or eat their dinner. Despite any attempts to double down with punishments, bribes, and physical force, we cannot actually make our children do what they don't want to do. We are not the boss of our children; they are the boss of themselves.

Understanding this can be scary, but also incredibly freeing. Tiger parenting creates an antagonistic relationship with our children as we try to exert control over them, but when we untiger and stop trying to be our child's boss, we take the boot off their necks and eliminate the root of a lot of power struggles and conflicts. The flailing and fighting slowly disappear because the oppressive pressure has been removed. Peace and trust can be restored when our young people know that we are willing to honor their autonomy and agency. Instead of relying on restrictions and rules, we lean into *respect* and *relationship*.

Food

Food is a huge part of Chinese culture, but it is also an aspect of family life that is often fraught with control and conflict. Children (and adults!) are often encouraged to eat past the point of fullness to please the parent or the host, or are shamed for eating at all if they are considered overweight. I grew up being expected to finish every single grain of rice in my bowl and consume whatever was placed in front of me without complaining. Such parental control and unhealthy attitudes toward food can unfortunately lead to disordered eating as we internalize these messages. Instead of listening to our bodies and intuition, we can easily become obsessed with controlling our eating to please others, avoid shame, or conform to social standards.

When my kids were young, I placed these same expectations on them and tried to shovel shiitake mushrooms and lentils down their throats faster than they could spit them up. But as they grew older, they learned to exercise their power to protest. One decided that he didn't like tofu and couldn't handle anything with even a hint of spice. The other loved all kinds of curry but preferred not to eat most raw vegetables. They were in agreement on how disgusting mushrooms were. Rather than fighting them on it and assuming that I knew better than they did about their own bodies, I started respecting their preferences and boundaries. If they told me they were full, I didn't overrule them and make them finish. If they picked out the eggplant, winter melon, or 木耳 (wood-ear mushroom), I didn't force them to eat it before they could leave the table. I listened to them.

Just as we adults exercise autonomy over what we eat, when we eat, and how much we eat, our children deserve the same. This is not to say that we give our young people a carte blanche and that there are no boundaries around food. Every family has to consider finances, medical restrictions, sensory/food sensitivities, preferences, and priorities, but there's almost always a way to approach things through the filter of relationship and respect.

For example, it's an important family ritual for us to share dinners together at the table (relationship), but no one is ever forced to eat or finish their food (respect). The kids are free to snack on whatever is in the pantry (respect), but we ask them to consider others before finishing the whole Costco bag of dried mangoes in one go (relationship). I try to prepare meals that we all enjoy (relationship), but they're free to make themselves something else if they're not happy with the choices (respect).

This can start even at a young age, where we allow our kids to feed themselves instead of spoon-feeding them. It may be messy in the short run, but the long-term payoffs of competence and autonomy are worth it. As they get older, we can enlist their help in planning and preparing meals so they have a say and investment in the process. Eating family-style, as many Asians do, is actually quite conducive to bodily autonomy and relationship. This form of sharing a meal together can honor both these values when we offer a variety of dishes from which our kids can pick and choose. Instead of plating their food for them or deciding how much they are required to eat, they can fill their own bowls and control their own portions. As they practice attuning to their bodies, they will become more discerning about what to eat and how much to eat in a way that feels good to them.

Watching us appreciate and enjoy a variety of foods without forcing it upon them or withholding it from them can also encourage our young people to become more adventurous eaters and inoculate them against negative messages about food. They are more inclined to try new things and listen to their bodies instead of simply reacting to our control. They may be less drawn to overindulging in "taboo" foods because the options provided for them aren't taboo at all. Of course, this does not guarantee that our kids will be "good eaters," but removing the coercive element around food will allow them to practice more intuitive eating.

When we apply these principles of the personal and the communal—the consideration of our own bodies along with consideration of others—our dinner tables no longer have to be battlefields.

Physical Affection

Honoring consent and the bodily autonomy of our kids is especially relevant as we consider how often these are violated by those in power. Women are often expected to smile pretty or respond gratefully to men's attentions, whether welcomed or not. Likewise, children are forced to give hugs, offer kisses, and endure tickles against their will. When we rob our kids of their agency to decide how they want to use their bodies, we inadvertently make them vulnerable to sexual abuse. They are accustomed to their bodies being used to please others. However, when we empower them to say, "No," "Stop," "I don't like that," and actually respect their boundaries, they learn to be attuned to their own sensations and confident in their own power.

Because physical affection is only meaningful when it is enthusiastically and authentically offered, we need to always ask for a child's consent and remove any pressure for them to show us affection. This can start at an early age. Babies make it clear when they don't like being tossed in the air or rubbed with scruffy facial hair. We need to listen to them. Toddlers will let you know when they want to run around and play instead of snuggling with you. We need to respect them instead of centering our own egos.

I have a three-year-old niece who takes a while to warm up to people. While it's tempting for me to scoop her up and smother her with kisses the moment I see her, I try to give her the space she needs. I make myself available to play with her or offer to read a book. I don't take offense when she says no. I ask permission to hold her hand, or carry her, or give her a kiss. If she pushes away, turns her head, or hides behind her mom, I don't insist on it. I've found that when we exude warmth and honor towards children, they learn to trust us; they know that we will respect their boundaries, and often end up naturally expressing affection on their own terms.

The benefits are not limited to protection against abuse. When children are empowered to listen to their bodies, they are not only able to express what brings them pain and discomfort, but also what brings them pleasure. "Yes." "More." "I like that." One child may like it when you scratch their back. Another may prefer tight bear hugs. Every child is different and enjoys different sensations. When we listen to their preferences, they feel a sense of embodiment and agency over their own bodies. This lays the groundwork for healthy communication as they develop and explore physical pleasure that feels right for them.

All that being said, we as parents also have the right to bodily autonomy. While we *respect* our children's boundaries, the *relational* aspect means that we don't ignore our own needs either. Mothers in particular often complain of being touched out. Offering breast-feeding, physical affection, and nurturing to our children out of obligation and without our consent and enjoyment is just another way that women are taught to please others at our own expense. While we want to do our best to make sure our children's needs are met, I also believe that setting boundaries around our own bodies is completely appropriate. It serves no one for us to ignore our own needs and grow resentful. Requiring our consent and drawing boundaries teaches our children that we are not vending machines at their disposal. We are whole people.

I have one child who is particularly affectionate. When he was younger, he loved my bare arms—kissing them, stroking them, squeezing and "chubbying" them. Whenever warm weather hit and

I found myself in a short-sleeve shirt, he was like a shark smelling blood in the water, homing in on my exposed flesh. I felt smothered and overwhelmed by his ravenous affection. It finally got to the point where I had to tell him to first ask for my permission. "I don't like it when you just grab my arm and go to town on it. I feel like you're using my body. Please ask me first if you can kiss me."

While this may seem harsh, setting such boundaries teaches an important lesson about consent, especially for boys who are conditioned to believe that they can use women's bodies for their own enjoyment. It reminds them that other people's needs and boundaries are just as important as their own. For me, communicating this boundary helped me feel more in control of my own body. Because I felt less manipulated and resentful, I found I was more emotionally available and able to show affection to my son when he needed it. Because I cared about his desire for affection and sensory input, I found other ways to get his needs met. We gave him a fuzzy blanket to sleep with. We adopted a cat for him to snuggle with. We got him squishy toys to squeeze.

When we consider both the principles of *respect* and *relationship*, we can almost always find creative ways to meet everyone's needs and honor everyone involved.

Appearance

When our children are young, we often treat them like baby dolls, dressing them up in cute little suits, frilly dresses, or whatever adorable outfit we can find. We view their appearance as an extension of ourselves and our style (or in my case, lack thereof). While dressing our children is considered an inalienable parental right, it is also a way that we rob our children of autonomy over their bodies, especially when they dissent. Little babies might express discomfort over itchy material, toddlers might resist wearing their Sunday best, and teenagers might defy our rules of modesty, yet we often ignore their complaints or preferences for the sake of taking a picture-perfect family photo or impressing our friends. In our attempts to maintain our own image and ego, we violate our children's sovereignty over their own bodies.

I have tried to encourage one of my children to try a new hair-style—one that, in my opinion, is cooler and more flattering. He refuses to stray from his standard crew cut. He doesn't want a lot of fuss and unwelcome attention. He doesn't like dramatic change. I've realized that I need to back off and respect his wishes instead of pressuring him to be someone he isn't. His body, his choice. My other child likes comfortable and casual clothes. He has not worn jeans in several years and only recently got sneakers that weren't Velcro. He often wears his pants and shorts backwards, shrugging indifferently when I point it out.

While I sometimes wish both my kids would take more care about the way they look, I know that that's my issue, not theirs. Their appearance is an expression of who they are as people and how they want to manifest themselves in the world. What right have I to decide that for them? Respecting our children's autonomy means we teach them to be in tune with their bodies and themselves instead of mindlessly following the latest trend, wearing the most popular brand, or dressing simply to please others.

The opposite is true as well: some children are particular about their appearance and have very sophisticated tastes. Some may be fascinated with fashion, hair, makeup, piercings, tattoos, or gen-der-bending. While these may not reflect our personal values or preferences, we need not demonize them either. They may reflect a young person's artistic nature, passionate temperament, or indepen-dent spirit. I'm not saying that we should give in to their every whim, but as parents we can approach these conversations with sensitiv-ity rather than judgment. We can listen with open hearts to what they find appealing and express our desire to honor their autonomy, even while we discuss our concerns about health risks, peer pressure, and being overly image-conscious. Instead of trying to control and police their appearance, we can find safe and age-appropriate ways to honor their experimentation and self-discovery.

When we prioritize respecting our kids' autonomy, it opens the door for discussion about what may be appropriate for different settings, culturally sensitive, or considerate towards others. This is the relational part. Running around naked may be fine at home, but perhaps not welcome at the fancy restaurant. They might want to wear their favorite white dress to the Lunar New Year party, but—being the color of death and mourning in Chinese culture—it would probably be offensive to the grandparents. They may love a certain T-shirt, but I might point out the misogynistic message of the graphic and ask them to reconsider. When the foundation of respect and relationship has been laid, mutual give-and-take will naturally take place out of love, trust, and consideration for one another.

When we learn to love our children as they are, no matter what, their appearance no longer becomes a source of shame or vanity for us. It becomes just another source of delight as we continue to discover who they are and how they want to show up in the world.

While the specifics of creating a culture of consent will look different for every family, *respect* and *relationship* are foundational. These are general principles that can be applied to pretty much every aspect of family life: hygiene, sleep, screen time, etc. The key is to honor your child's bodily autonomy while building connection, trust, and communication. As we model these values, our children will not only learn to confidently embody themselves; they will learn to draw healthy boundaries and honor others' boundaries as well.

PART 4

RECOGNIZING OUR THREATS

very good zoologist knows that when an animal population shows decline or disease, environmental factors need to be taken into consideration. Often, it's due to human impact through poaching, encroachment on their natural habitat, pollution of their food and water sources, or poisoning their prey. Yet when humans make a concerted effort to protect the environment and engage in animal conservation, animals can often be brought back from the brink of extinction.

Likewise, we need to take a step back and consider how our social ecosystem is affecting the healthy growth and development of our children. Children face many social pressures and environmental stresses—school, social media, economic instability, ineffective government, and climate change (just to name a few)—which cause a host of physical, psychological, and relational problems. Yet we often put the burden upon individuals and family units to deal personally with the issues instead of considering how we as a society can work together to course correct.

Untigering is, therefore, not just about changing our internal dialogue or transforming the dynamics of our family relationships. We can't escape the influence of the world around us by simply trying to create a safe and loving bubble inside our homes. We need to understand how the threats that exist in our greater social and cultural context can affect the well-being of our children. Parenting is not private and personal; it is inherently social and political.

I saw this at play when my child started expressing anxiety about his body. In my home, I try to avoid diets, the scale, negative body talk, and demonizing food. I try to speak lovingly about our bodies, including my own. But countless comments by friends and family members who straight up told my son that he was fat ("哇，胖了!") had seeped in and he had become self-conscious. A visit to the doctor only heaped on more shame as she pointed out his weight gain and encouraged him to lay off junk food. A few days later, he

admitted to me that he had watched a video for ways to lose weight.
He was only 9 years old.

It both broke my heart and angered me to know that my care-free little boy developed body image issues because of the messaging he received from the world around him.

If we are to help our children thrive in this world, we have to be aware of the hazards and perils that exist in the environment. We have to teach them where there are snares and where to find shelter, who is a friend and who is a predator, what to consume and what to abstain from. If we are not aware of how societal values and norms affect our parenting, we will be swept along by the tides, blindsided by the challenges we face when we live and parent counter-cultur-ally. If, however, we open our eyes and are alert to the realities of our surroundings, we can avoid the pitfalls and help create change.

In this section, I will address different social and cultural beliefs that create obstacles and threats for us as we untiger, specifically with a Chinese American lens that challenges both Western and Chinese attitudes. A deep dive into larger social issues like racism, social media, the environment, or capitalism go beyond the scope of this book, but it is my hope that as we become more aware of the toxic elements in our society, we can work together for social change so that our values are represented both inside and outside our homes.

CHAPTER 18

THE MYTH OF MERITOCRACY

My parents arrived in America with the equivalent of less than $300 in their pockets. My dad studied full-time for his master's degree while working part-time as a window cleaner and security guard, scraping together enough money to survive and even send money home to his parents in Hong Kong as the dutiful firstborn son. My mother worked odd jobs with her limited English, changing the diapers of both the babies and the elderly she was hired to care for.

Navigating life in a foreign land and in a foreign language was no small feat, but through their grit and hard work they were able to provide a safe and stable home for my siblings and me, free of many of the struggles that they had experienced growing up. Just one generation later, my sister and brother-in-law are founders of a global software company, boasting clients like Coach, Volkswagen, and T-Mobile. My brother co-owns a clothing brand with a celebrity following that has been featured in magazines like *GQ*, *Hypebeast*, and *Forbes*. As for me, I'm currently unemployed... but that's another story.

This immigrant narrative of fulfilling the rags-to-riches American dream is not uncommon. Many arrive to the "land of opportunity" as penniless immigrants and are able to find success and prosperity. Unlike China, where 关系 guanxi (social networks and connections) is needed to open doors and opportunities, in America it's possible to advance and achieve success on the strength of hard work and merit alone.

There's just one problem with that story.

It's not true.

We may believe that we are self-made people, but in reality, there are social, political, and systemic forces that serve as the gatekeepers of success. When we presume that we've earned educational opportunities, financial prosperity, and professional achievement solely on our merit, we fall for the fairy tale of our own heroism and fail to recognize the privileges that have contributed to our achievements. We not only delude ourselves about our greatness, but also judge others who seem less accomplished.

The Paradox of Meritocracy

Meritocracy is a myth—and a particularly insidious one— because it seeks to maintain power dynamics and social rankings even while claiming to dismantle them. It is presented as a solution to fixed hierarchies based on birth, class, or race, promising the chance of upward mobility based on our natural talent and determination. Yet as much as it claims to be the great equalizer, the reality is that meritocracy actually upholds and perpetuates inequality. It gives people the illusion that the world is fair and just, professing impartiality while ignoring systemic injustices and implicit biases that favor men over women, rich over poor, white over people of color, and certain ethnic groups over others.

Emilio Castilla, professor of management at MIT, has studied how meritocratic ideals affect the way companies treat their employees.[52] Surprisingly, he found that meritocracy had the opposite of its intended effect. Organizations that explicitly valued meritocracy ended up showing greater preference towards white men, rewarding them with higher salary increases over women, ethnic minorities, and those born outside the U.S. despite all other factors being equal, including their performance scores.

This "paradox of meritocracy" shows how assumed objectivity actually leads to discrimination. Managers and leaders, believing themselves to be fair and impartial, fail to acknowledge their own unconscious biases and stereotypes about gender, education, ethnicity, disability, etc. By ignoring how their filters influence their evaluations and claiming that their judgments are unbiased, they serve to maintain the existing social order that favors white men and disadvantages the marginalized.

Those who are awarded, promoted, and given opportunities believe that they have earned their place, unaware of the privileges and circumstances that have paved the way for them. They congratulate themselves for coming out ahead and condemn others for losing a race that's actually rigged from the beginning. Instead of challenging broken systems, they help perpetuate them.

Those who are unable to climb the ladders of success because of systemic oppression begin to doubt themselves. If the system is fair, then their inability to get ahead must be due to their own incompetence. This negative effect of meritocracy can be observed in marginalized groups even at a young age. Children of color who experience discrimination and racial injustice—yet trust that they're only getting what they deserve—internalize negative stereotypes about themselves that affect their self-esteem and lead to risky behaviors.[53] Instead of recognizing that there are a host of injustices and environmental factors that contribute to the problem, they believe that they are the problem.

Meritocracy and Asian Americans

As Asian Americans, many of us have benefited from this myth of meritocracy and its close cousin, the "model minority"[54] stereotype. Asian Americans are perceived to be a monolithic people who are all smart, hard-working, upstanding citizens who hold good jobs and have good families. While this stereotype grossly misrepresents such a diverse demographic, many of us have unwittingly leveraged it for our own advantage, achieving a measure of success and prosperity that we attribute solely to our work ethic. We flatter ourselves with fantasies of pulling ourselves up by our bootstraps instead of acknowledging how immigration policies, preferential hiring practices, government support, and positive stereotypes have worked in our favor to provide many of us with certain privileges and opportunities not afforded to other people of color.

I just learned not long ago that my parents' first home in Canada was built on land that was given to us by the government. The city wanted to encourage development in a new neighborhood and offered plots of land for free. My mother, who was doing data entry for the municipal government at the time, heard about the housing assistance program through the grapevine and knew that this was a rare opportunity. She applied early and we were quickly approved. This whole time, I had thought my parents' ability to own a home and build wealth was because of their hard work, perseverance, and wise money management. The reality is that government support and being at the right place at the right time were large factors as well. The belief in meritocracy causes us to focus on our own efforts while ignoring outside factors that contribute to our success.

First-generation immigrants of all ethnicities often have a vested belief in meritocracy. Compared to the injustice and oppression they witnessed in their home countries, America is a veritable treasure trove of opportunity and upward mobility. The ideals of meritocracy, democracy, and freedom are woven into the mythology of America that drives immigration—it compels people to traverse oceans and mountains, leave family and friends, and put their lives on the line for a taste of that good life. Meritocracy thus becomes a beacon of hope and a chance at a better life. They'd rather continue to chase that dream than admit that it's all a mirage.

On the other hand, the new wave of immigrants from China often come from wealth and privilege. Because they did well for themselves even back in their home countries, they are often pro-China, politically and fiscally conservative, and invested in the myth of meritocracy. They're not interested in challenging a power structure that they have benefited from.

Second-generation immigrants and subsequent generations often have a different perspective. Not having grown up in other social and political contexts, our eyes are wide open to the systemic injustice that we see and experience in America without needing to compare it with how bad it was back in _____ (name of other country). We are not soothed by the reminder of how good we have it or by the promise of "bread and circuses" when we see how much work there still is to be done. Our relationships go beyond the tight ethnic enclaves that our immigrant parents found refuge in, and we are more informed about the white supremacy, colonialism, racism, and patriarchy our government and institutions were founded on. We see through the veneer of meritocracy.

Meritocracy and Tiger Parenting

At the core of tiger parenting is the belief in meritocracy: hard work pays off, we are the makers of our own destiny, and our achievements are a reflection of our character and worth. The goal is to raise competitive and successful children by whatever means necessary.

The objective is to teach them to both fit the mold *and* stand out in an effort to become the ideal college applicant. Those who rise to the top are entitled to their ascendancy; those who don't make the cut are simply lazy and inadequate. This toxic culture of competition and dominance breeds arrogance and destroys empathy. It drives our children to one-upmanship as they feverishly try to prove themselves and keep ahead of the curve. Despite its alluring promises, meritocracy comes at a great cost to our children's mental and emotional health, well-being, and relationships with others.

As parents, we have to recognize that meritocracy is a fantasy, concocted by the powers that be in order to keep us fighting amongst ourselves for the crumbs at the foot of their table. It serves only to favor those already at the top rather than offering a way up for those at the bottom. Exposing the lie of meritocracy pulls back the curtain on the systemic injustices upon which America was built.

We can refuse to uphold this false narrative. We can dig deeper into our own histories to peel back the layers of privilege that have helped us get to where we are. Doing so can grant us gratitude and humility regarding our achievements and prompt us to ensure that others receive those same benefits.

We can examine our national lore and expose how systems are built to maintain inequity and the status quo. We can decolonize education and question the stories of white supremacy and American exceptionalism. We can teach our children the histories that have been deliberately silenced or ignored.

We can divest ourselves of the beliefs and systems that force our children to battle it out for top dog status. Instead, we can teach them that they are loved and worthy, apart from any merits or demerits they might have in the world's eyes. We can de-emphasize grades, elite universities, exclusive clubs, and competitive internships—institutional constructs that require our children to make enemies and rivals of one another when they could just as easily be collaborators and friends. Our children may not be able to avoid participating in these systems, but they can do so as an authentic expression of their intrinsic desires rather than as a means to best others or feed their own egos.

Meritocracy is a myth. The game is rigged. We can refuse to offer our children up as tribute.

CHAPTER 19

PERMISSIVENESS

A s a child of strict Chinese parents, I often criticize the coercive authoritarian parenting that I grew up with and practiced for many years. But if I'm honest, I find permissive parenting equally problematic.

While archetypal tiger parenting gives the parents all the power, permissive parenting hands over all the power to the kids. Responsibility to guide and set loving limits is abdicated. "No" is a taboo word. Boundaries are almost nonexistent. This kind of parenting may seem gentle, but it is not loving. It's nice, but not kind. Love has boundaries and limits. It requires us to intervene, to prevent harm, and to teach our kids appropriate ways to get their needs met.

When parents fail to offer guidance or draw consistent, loving boundaries, children often grow up lacking the skills to:

- **Regulate their emotions or behavior.** They have a harder time with impulse control because they are rarely given limits. They may struggle with emotional self-regulation because parents leave them to work out things on their own or rescue them from unpleasant feelings and situations.

- **Respect others**. Since their feelings, needs, and desires are always centered, they are not taught to empathize and consider others. Unaware and indifferent to the effects of their choices, they may bulldoze and bully to get what they want.
- **Take responsibility and repair**. Children of permissive parents are not taught to own their mistakes and make things right. Instead, they are given a pass for their harmful or inappropriate behavior.

This happens when our daughter bites another kid and all we do is explain defensively, "She's teething." When our son whacks another child playfully and we just laugh and say, "Boys will be boys." When our child pulls a Veruca Salt[55] in the store and we placate her by promising, "Don't worry, sweetie. I'll get you whatever you want." These are all ways we absolve our children and ourselves from respecting the boundaries and limits of relationships and resources. When we only consider our child's need for respect and autonomy without teaching them to extend the same consideration to others, we breed entitlement and egocentrism. Our children are left without any guidance about how to control their impulses, redirect their energies, or empathize with others.

While this is detrimental to the personal well-being of our children and the peace within our homes, it can be devastating—and even deadly—when we view it from a social justice standpoint. Overlooking harmful behavior can create individuals who dominate and violate boundaries. Indulging and making allowances for our child's every whim ignores how those freedoms may infringe upon others. Authoritarianism is not the only way we teach children to become oppressors. Permissiveness can be just as effective because it allows bad behavior to go unchecked.

I see this so clearly during this COVID-19 pandemic. Individuals who flaunt the shelter-in-place guidelines to go off to vacation, parties, or other non-essential activities are clearly not practiced in understanding the ramifications of their actions upon others. As a nation, Americans are not used to hearing "No" or curbing their personal freedoms for the good of the whole. This crisis has gone far in exposing the disparity between the haves and the have-nots, whether that's access to health care or toilet paper. Sadly, in this case, such entitled behavior will very likely lead to great suffering and fatalities.

We can see this destructive behavior play out in other areas of society:

- Young men are taught to affirm their sexuality and physicality, but not taught to honor sexual consent or tame their aggression.
- The wealthy freely pursue their own comfort but are unwilling to give up privilege so that others have access to services and resources.
- White people openly express their fears and tears yet disregard how doing so actually endangers the lives of Black and brown people.
- Those with power and privilege are shown "forgiveness" and leniency but are rarely held accountable for the harm they've caused. Their feelings are prioritized over those they've victimized.
- Powerful nations and corporations carelessly consume resources or destroy the environment without considering the ramifications for present and future generations.
- Those who are homophobic/transphobic are more concerned about their right to free speech than they are about how their hateful words affect the LGBTQIA community.

Focusing on the freedom of the individual without regard for the social implications is myopic and irresponsible. It ignores the inequalities embedded into our systems where certain individuals (usually the rich, white, heterosexual male ones) are afforded opportunities and compassion while others are not. Laissez-faire parenting leads to laissez-faire politics where protecting personal rights is deemed more important than considering what's best for the whole community and our shared life together.

But lest we think that permissiveness is exclusively a problem with Western "white parenting," we must acknowledge that permissiveness is also widespread in Chinese culture—from the favoring and coddling of sons over daughters to the rise of overindulged "little emperors"[56] as a result of China's one-child policy and the scandalous antics of the 富二代 *fu er dai*[57] (children of China's nouveau riche). Whatever the cultural context, such examples show how indulged individuals can grow up to become oppressors who terrorize those around them, just like Dudley,[58] Harry Potter's spoiled cousin.

In many ways, permissiveness is even more insidious than authoritarianism because its harmful effects are masked behind a smile. Ideals like respect, empathy, and freedom are twisted to excuse bad behavior and ignore accountability. As peaceful parents, our passion for liberation and love needs to extend beyond the four walls of our home and out into our community. What we desire for our children, we must desire for *all* children. While we refuse to take up the heavy-handed cudgel of coercive parenting, authoritarian government, or heavy policing, we must likewise reject the reckless magic wand of permissive parenting that can too easily be used as a tool to uphold injustice, white supremacy, patriarchy, and other forms of oppression.

Peaceful parenting calls us to love and validate our children; to understand their developmental needs and let go of unfair expectations; to give them space to express themselves and exercise their autonomy; to respect and honor them.

But if we stop there, we are still complicit in oppression.

Tolerance without teaching is dangerous. Taking seriously our practice of anti-oppression means we must also lovingly limit, guide, and equip our children so that they learn how to respect and honor others. Otherwise, the liberty we offer our children easily turns into license, and the autonomy that we safeguard for them ends up enabling abuse.

CHAPTER 20

FILIAL PIETY

The foundation of most Chinese family relationships is 孝 *xiao*, or filial piety. It's the Confucian virtue of respecting your parents and elders. Parents are expected to direct, train, discipline, and provide for the next generation. Children, in turn, are expected to obey, honor, serve, and care for their parents.

Sounds good... but is it really?

Let's admit it—for a moral code that is supposed to produce familial harmony, filial piety too often leads to resentment, rebellion, and even estrangement. That's because filial piety is rooted in some problematic dynamics.

Filial Piety is Respect Based on Power

Those with more power command respect from those with less: parents over children, men over women, those with rank over those without. For the child, compliance is required in matters as trivial as being told to put on a jacket in 90 degree weather, to something as weighty as deferring to your parents about who to marry. Filial piety is, more often than not, weaponized by the powerful to keep the powerless in check.

But we live in a world that is moving away from ancient hierarchical structures toward more equitable relationships. Wives no longer walk five steps behind their husbands. Children are now actually allowed to speak at the dinner table. The growing access to personal power means that kids nowadays do not submit to their parents "just because." Parents can no longer use their positions of authority to control their kids without enduring constant power struggles or resorting to increasingly coercive and abusive means.

Filial Piety is Respect Based on Duty

Filial piety is behavior that is motivated by obligation. It's the oppressive power of "should."

Many believe that having an internal sense of duty is good, but Alfie Kohn, in his book *The Myth of the Spoiled Child*, disagrees:

> Children who have introjected commands [internalized someone else's rules or standards] to be polite or dutiful or helpful are not really moral agents in any meaningful sense. They haven't chosen to do good because they don't experience themselves as choosing. After all, ensuring that children internalize our values isn't the same thing as helping them to develop their own.[59]

Children who are driven by duty may end up doing the right thing, but they do so at the risk of losing their own agency, sense of self, and internal moral compass. They become people who are good at following the rules, but unable to thoughtfully examine and challenge unjust systems.

Filial Piety is Respect Based on Idealism

Everything goes smoothly as long as everyone plays their appropriate roles. Parents raise and provide for their children sacrificially, and in response children owe them honor and obedience.

Unfortunately, while filial piety may work well in a perfect family, I'm guessing none of us actually have one of those. In the real world, human relationships are complex. Both parents and children inevitably disappoint one another. Filial respect fails to recognize this dynamism and messiness. It relies on strict adherence to social expectations, but completely breaks down when someone breaks the rules.

Filial Piety is Respect Based on Fear

When duty fails to motivate children to obey, there's always fear. Parents call for absolute compliance for fear of losing face and losing control. Children choose to comply out of fear of disapproval, punishment, and conflict. But in the words of Albert Camus, "Nothing is more despicable than respect based on fear."[60]

Fear does not create an environment that fosters healthy, flourishing families. It causes children to feel deeply insecure about their parents' love. Even when children are well-behaved, they are never quite sure if their parents' acceptance is unconditional or dependent on their acquiescence.

Filial piety, while cloaked in respectability and morality, proves highly questionable when it has been invoked by tiger parents around the world to coerce, shame, and instill fear in their children.

True Respect

True respect is not something that can be demanded. It's not something that is owed simply because of title, position, or social obligation. It is not merely an expectation of outward compliance. True respect is offered freely when we genuinely esteem and value another person. It is earned through love and trust. It is an expression of heartfelt devotion. **True respect is what we show *to* our children before we can expect it *from* them.**

As an untigering mom, I absolutely want respect in my family relationships. But I don't want filial piety. I want something better, truer, and sounder—a mutual respect that is characterized by shared power, offered without coercion, rooted in authenticity, and fostered through unconditional love.

Now that's the kind of foundation that's worth building on.

CHAPTER 21

TRANSACTIONAL RELATIONSHIPS

The Chinese are nothing if not supremely practical in relationships. Built on a framework of reciprocity and mutuality, relationships are always viewed through the lens of ROI (return on investment).

Careful note is taken of how much red envelope money is received so it can be reciprocated accordingly. A favor is given with the expectation that the recipient will return the favor at a future date. A boyfriend is only considered potential husband material if he can provide you with a home and steady income.

Never is this truer than when it comes to the relationship between parent and child. Parents often treat children as investments with an expected return.

I'm taking care of you now. I expect you to take care of me when I get older.

I'm paying for your college tuition, so you'd better make something of yourself.

I sacrificed everything to give you a better life. You owe me.

Such relational economics work well when children dutifully meet parental expectations. But what happens when they don't? I can recount too many stories of those who incurred the fiery wrath or the icy silence of their parents when they dared to forge their own way—pursuing a career their parents deemed unworthy, marrying someone their parents considered unsuitable... pretty much doing anything that went against their parents' wishes. With so many conditions attached, it's no wonder that such parental "investment" becomes a tool of manipulation instead of a means of empowerment; a burden that saddles children down instead of wings that help them fly.

Those of us who are untigering need to dismantle this transactional view of relationships. Whether with our parents or with our children, we need to refuse to engage in conditional expressions of love—love that is only given with the thought of what the other owes; love that is only offered when something can be personally gained.

Scrambled Eggs and Tears for Breakfast

For the past several years, our family's Sunday morning ritual has been for the parents to sleep in while the kids make breakfast. Noah is in charge of making the bacon and Caleb is responsible for cooking the scrambled eggs. It's a sweet deal for Jason and I, but it all fell apart one particular morning when Noah woke up not feeling well. He asked if I could do the bacon and I, of course, agreed, shooing him back into bed so he could get more rest.

The minute Caleb found out, the complaining began.

> *"Why do I have to cook the eggs when 哥哥 isn't making the bacon?"*
> *"It's not fair that 哥哥's not doing anything!"*

On and on it went. I felt my temperature rising. I was annoyed at his self-centeredness and irritated by his pettiness. I finally snapped and yelled, "Forget it! I'll just do it myself!"

I banged around the kitchen angrily as I cooked the bacon, scrambled the eggs, toasted the bread, put away the dishes, washed the dishes, set the table, made fresh soy milk, and brewed tea for my Hong Kong 奶茶, all the while fuming as I thought, "Why am I the only one doing anything while everyone else is sitting on their butts?!" I was almost in tears at the unfairness of it all.

That's when it hit me. The thing that I expected of my children was the very thing I was unable to do myself: give without expecting something in return.

As a full-time homemaker, I naturally do a lot for my family. But I rarely do so willingly, joyfully, or lovingly. I do it out of duty and expectation. I feel that I have no choice. The needs of my family are not opportunities; they are demands. My household tasks are not free gifts of service that I offer; they are jobs that are required of me. I expect reciprocity and fair compensation for my labor, only I don't get paid. *I'm always in the red.* Capitalism has colonized my view of relationships and I see things only in terms of debt, credit, and the balance sheet. There is no room for gifts of grace and generosity in such an economy.

Especially for women and mothers, we internalize so many expectations, whether real or perceived. We get the job done, and— since we're overachieving tiger parents—we do it well. But when we live out of obligation, it feels like a burden; when we only give expecting something in return, we become resentful when our kids don't reciprocate or show us appreciation.

I realized that if I truly wanted my family to embody the values of unconditional love, I had to dismantle my capitalist mindset built upon scarcity, contracts, and payments for services rendered. Instead, I needed to pursue the values of a gift economy, where giving and receiving are done freely, joyfully, and without coercion. This meant that I had to stop trying to play the martyr mother role and be honest about my own boundaries. I had to unplug from the sense of duty so I could tap into my heartfelt desires. I had to be free to say "No" so that I could truly say "Yes." And I had to give that same choice to my kids.

That same afternoon, we had a family meeting. We informed Noah and Caleb that they were no longer required to do chores. Oh, they were still responsible for personal tasks like making their bed and putting away their laundry, but they were not obligated to take on any family responsibilities. Instead, we encouraged them to have a team mentality, keeping their eyes open for ways they could be thoughtful and helpful. Together, we brainstormed a list of possible ways they could serve the family and then posted it up on the fridge. No assigned chores. No expectations. Just an invitation for each one of us to contribute to the family willingly and cheerfully.

It's been several years since we started living out the values of a gift economy. While it's not the most efficient (few things based on connection are) and I am sometimes prone to falling back into those transactional ways of relating, the results have been transformative for our family. Jason and I ask for the kids' help around the house if we need it, but we also gladly serve them when they're engrossed in a game, online chat, book, or project. Noah often offers to help with dinner and regularly asks me, "Is there anything I can help with?" Every morning, Caleb puts away the clean dishes without us asking. He even makes scrambled eggs every Sunday for us all without complaint, bacon or no bacon. We're discovering the joy that comes from freely sharing our gifts with one another without expecting something in return.

Unconditional love compels us to support, serve, and resource our children for their sake, not ours. We give because we see their potential, sacrifice because we desire their thriving, provide because we want to empower them to achieve their goals... not because we need them to pay us back, stroke our egos, scratch our backs, or give us face. Parenting without expecting a return means that we give freely, love unconditionally, and respect the choices that our kids make. The beautiful irony of this unconditional kind of parenting? We ultimately end up with the most valuable ROI of all: our children's trust, love, and flourishing... no strings attached.

CHAPTER 22

SAVING FACE

The concept of 面子 *mianzi*, or "face," is deeply embedded in Chinese culture. While there is not really a Western equivalent, face can be understood as "dignity" or "reputation"—the positive regard and honor one has in the eyes of others, the avoidance of shame and public embarrassment.

Imagine it as a kind of social currency that can be saved, lost, or given. Saving face requires us to do what is socially expected of us— playing by the rules and presenting a positive image of ourselves. Even if it means breaking the bank by throwing a wedding banquet we can't afford or crushing our souls by pretending our marriage is perfect, we do so to maintain our respectability.

Losing face occurs whenever our weaknesses or failings are brought to light in public. Openly disagreeing or criticizing someone, airing out dirty laundry, or writing a book critiquing the way you were raised are all face-losing situations that should be avoided at all cost.

Giving face means that we help maintain or improve another's standing in the eyes of others. Effusively praising someone in front of others, deferring to our elders, or giving our parents bragging rights for being accepted into an Ivy League school are all examples of giving face.

By now, you can probably tell how I feel about face by my sarcasm. You can chalk it up to my Western upbringing, but I'm not the only one. The younger generations in China are also tired of the exhausting rituals of saving face.[61] For those of us seeking to untiger, face ultimately gets in the way of our healing and transformation.

Saving Face Is Rooted in Insecurity

Instead of the unconditional regard and acceptance we and our children need, saving face teaches us that our worth is dependent on what others think. When our worth is defined by our standing in others' eyes, this is shaky ground indeed. Rather than being present and connected to ourselves, we stand outside of ourselves, always aware of how our words and our actions are being interpreted by others. We give our power away and allow others to control us.

This leads to deep insecurity and internalized shame. We become easily offended whenever there is a perceived slight. Our lives are not worth living if we face a business failure or a bad score on the college entrance exam. When we are not safe and settled in our absolute worth and worthiness, we are at the mercy of the shifting sands of public opinion.

Saving Face Makes Us Two-faced

Face teaches us to wear a mask and present to the world what it wants to see. It forces us to hide our true selves. We must appear generous even though we feel resentful. We must be cheerful even though we feel depressed. We must defer to our elders even when we disagree. It's an exhausting charade to keep up.

But just because it's a cultural norm doesn't mean that we need to buy into it. While in China, I was part of a spiritual community that really tried to fight the urge to save face. Our ethos was one of unconditional love and acceptance, something radically profound for those growing up in a culture where everyone is jockeying for position and prestige. In this safe space, we could admit our weaknesses and dare to be seen for who we really were. People felt free to be real and vulnerable. Many said that it was the only place where they could take off their masks.

Losing Face is Freeing

Even if we are entrenched in a culture that places undue value on status and people-pleasing, we can refuse to play by the same rules. We can prioritize our own values rather than subjecting ourselves to the social pressures that hold little meaning for us.

While living in China, I saw how our social capital as foreigners declined over the years. We arrived in 2003 as the rich "foreign experts," but by the time I left in 2019, my local friend was the one driving the Tesla and I was the one rolling up in my jerry-rigged electric bike. Most of our friends were earning double Jason's salary. Whenever we came back to the States for the summer, we were stocking up on bulk packages of underwear and dried cranberries while our Chinese friends asked us to bring back Tiffany bracelets and Michael Kors handbags. All these could have felt like a loss of face, but Jason and I would often laugh about them. We were unapologetically living and loving our best life as our upwardly mobile friends looked on in bafflement and wonder.

Now, there's nothing wrong with liking beautiful things, but being willing to lose face means that our identity isn't tied up in the status symbols that society prescribes. We can enjoy things for their own sake rather than for the cool factor. Being willing to lose face means we don't take ourselves too seriously, we don't worry too much about impressing people, and we don't waste our energy on maintaining our image. It empowers us to live authentically from our own beliefs and priorities. We can create a life that is meaningful to us rather than blindly following along. Losing face frees us because we know we are loved apart from the opinions of others.

Losing Face is Empowering to Others

While this may seem counterintuitive, our willingness to lose face can actually give others the room to step up and realize their own power. When we choose not to stroke our own egos but instead ask for help and input, others learn that they also have gifts and insights to offer the world. By listening when our kids call us out as parents, admitting that we don't know all the answers as teachers, or inviting those we lead to problem-solve together, we share some of our power and privilege with others.

Our vulnerability and humility also open up doors for others to share their own struggles. It is an act of faith to share candidly about our fears and failures—to dare to lose face. Doing so invites others to honor our trust, and in turn assures them that we won't use their weaknesses against them. By taking the emotional risk of baring our souls, our necks, and our true faces, we encourage others that it's safe to show us their authentic, messy selves too.

Another way we can empower others is through our self-love and rejection of shame. While living in Asia, we would often vacation in Thailand. Unlike California beaches, these beaches were usually filled with Russian tourists who unabashedly strutted around in their bikinis and Speedos, regardless of their age, body shape, or lack of melanin. I found it rather freeing to watch them, so indifferent were they to submitting to the "beach body" standard. Seeing their lack of self-consciousness made me realize I didn't have to concern myself with other people's judgments either. I could play in the waves and build sandcastles with my boys, carefree and present instead of embarrassed about my body. When we flout the rules of face, we can inspire others to accept themselves as they are.

Give Face a Chance

While I *am* critical of saving face to protect our own reputation, I do believe there is a time and place for *giving* face. Especially for those like me who have relationships with those from a face-saving culture, it's important to be sensitive to culturally appropriate forms of communication and behavior.

When we go out to dinner, we can still offer our great-grandma the seat of honor, make sure our parents get a bowl of rice before we do, avoid public and personal attacks against weird Uncle Tim, and slip our credit card to the waiter to pay for the bill. We can teach our children what to say to greet relatives properly, how to allow others to go first before spinning the lazy Susan, and why they should refrain from taking the last piece of walnut shrimp. Doing so need not be out of a sense of duty or a desire to please others. We can do all these things freely and gladly simply out of love, kindness, and genuine respect.

Giving face is also not limited to our elders and superiors. In fact, it can be most powerful when offered to those with less power. We can show our children special honor. We can express appreciation for the contributions of our team members. We can share our platform and pass the mic to those who experience greater marginalization. These are all meaningful ways to give face and share our social capital.

When we learn to lose face and accept ourselves as we are, we model the type of vulnerability and authenticity we hope to foster in our children as well. Instead of reinforcing the pressures of maintaining image and reputation, we can empower our children to be their authentic selves. Let's challenge the cultural norm of *face* that too often forces our child's true self into hiding. Let's refuse to tie our child's worth to the opinions of others. Let's not force them to play the role of a marionette: a painted smile on their face, receiving admiration and recognition... but with strings attached. Instead, may our children know our unconditional positive regard[62] for them, no matter what they do or how they behave.

CHAPTER 23

EATING BITTERNESS

s recovering tiger parents, most of us value grit and tenacity in the face of adversity. We appreciate mottos like:

No pain, no gain.
What doesn't kill you makes you stronger.
If it doesn't hurt, you're doing it wrong.

The Chinese even have a special phrase for this bearing of hardship: 吃苦 *chiku.*

It's a phrase that literally means "to eat bitterness," and it's something that the Chinese have turned into an art and a virtue. The ability to endure and overcome all kinds of trials is regarded as a fundamental part of the Chinese character.

Whereas the American value of comfort often means the avoidance of pain, Chinese culture accepts suffering as a natural part of life. The first of the Four Noble Truths of Buddhism states this very thing: "All life is full of suffering, pain, and sorrow."[63] This has influenced Chinese cultural norms in response to suffering—we know how to survive; we know how to persevere; we know how to suffer. But the very virtue that helps us survive tragedy and adversity doesn't necessarily help us—or our children—thrive.

The ability to eat bitterness can also poison us.

It Infects our Bodies and Minds

Unlike most Westerners who express depression through psychological symptoms, Chinese people typically manifest it through their bodies. There is even a term coined for this phenomenon: "Chinese somatization."[64] Many Chinese tend to experience their suffering through headaches, insomnia, chronic pain, fatigue, etc. rather than emotional or mental distress.

It's no wonder that so many of us experience pain in our bodies when we are taught to "eat bitterness"—the very language used for suffering employs somatic imagery. Suffering must be consumed and absorbed. It's assimilated into our physical bodies. It's stored in our bellies, our backs, our bones.

But sooner or later, our bodies betray our pain. Whether it's physical or mental distress, the bitterness will manifest somehow.[65]

When we model this type of stoic tenacity for our children, they learn that tears and signs of weakness are not welcome. The only option is to choke down their anguish and hold their feelings inside. Since there is no safe outlet for their suffering, they internalize it and embody it through stomachaches, autoimmune diseases, anxiety, and other physical and mental health issues.

Eating bitterness is simply not healthy for us or our children. We have to find other ways to process pain so it doesn't metastasize in our bodies. Simply making room for grief, anguish, tears, and emotional breakdowns can go a long way towards teaching our kids how to walk through suffering rather than around it.

It Prevents Us from Seeking Relief

A research article[66] about Chinese beliefs and behaviors regarding pain cites several studies that illustrate this cultural value of stoicism. In one study of an ethnically diverse sample of 480 cancer patients, the Asian Americans were the ones who reported the lowest pain scores. Another study of Taiwanese cancer patients suggests a cultural acceptance of and high tolerance for pain.

But this very ability to withstand intense hardship also prevents many Chinese people from seeking help. We fool ourselves and those around us into thinking we are fine when we are in fact suffering.

Whether physical or psychological, we can't get timely support if we are not honest about our pain. If we attempt to eat bitterness and resist seeking out relief until the suffering becomes intolerable, we end up experiencing undue agony.

We say to ourselves,

> *"All marriages are hard."*
> *"My parents weren't that bad."*
> *"I can handle the pain."*

But then we end up divorced, depressed, or diseased. Many crises might well be avoided if we acknowledge our need for support and ask for help earlier.

Not only does eating bitterness harm us, it harms our children and our relationship with them. They hide their suffering from us because we tend to minimize pain. They know not to ask for help from us because we will just tell them to tough it out instead of getting them the treatment, counseling, or other assistance they need. We abandon our children to suffer in silence alone when we are too concerned about putting up a brave front and having a stiff upper lip.

It Keeps us Submissive

Since pain and sorrow are an expected part of life, when we suffer unjustly, this cultural value teaches us to simply keep our heads down and carry on. Many Chinese immigrants accept racism and condescension as part and parcel of the immigrant experience. There's no use complaining about it. Instead, beat them at their own game. Outperform. Outshine. Outlast.

But in doing so, we often end up tolerating injustice and becoming complicit in perpetuating oppression. We're not interested in dismantling these systems; only in gaming them. Eating bitterness may therefore help us overcome personal difficulties, but it doesn't inspire us to be agents of change for the greater good. It keeps us in a self-seeking, submissive survival mode that prevents us from addressing wrongs and speaking truth to power. When our kids see us modeling this, they also learn to not rock the boat. They learn to accept injustice or look away instead of naming it for what it is.

It Erodes Our Compassion

Eating bitterness can be a bit like surviving a hazing. We had to endure humiliation and abuse to make it into the inner circle. Now we expect other pledges to endure the same.

Those who flinch, faint, or falter provoke our derision instead of our compassion. When we believe all of us just need to suck it up, it's easy to look down on the "weak." Our ability to eat bitterness thus becomes a badge of honor instead of a way to connect and empathize with others who are suffering. Because we have not learned to grieve and process our own pain, there is no room in our hearts to carry anyone else's.

This extends to the way we treat our children. We have no patience or grace for their hardships or troubles. *You have it easy compared to what I went through! You're too soft, weak, coddled. So you didn't make the team; what's the big deal?* Sadly, our ability to muscle through has just made us hard towards those who are most vulnerable.

I appreciate the tenacity and resilience taught to me through my Chinese heritage. Eating bitterness has provided sustenance for my survival. It has fueled my ability to persevere in the face of unspeakable odds. It has contributed to my successes and achievements. **But there's a time for swallowing the bitterness down and there's a time for spitting it out.**

What we need for ourselves and for our children is not simply the ability to face hardship but the freedom to grieve, to cry, to vent, and to be weak. We need safe spaces where we can let the tears flow and let our guard down.

We must endure pain, but we must also learn to express pain. We need courage to deal with hardship, but we also need courage to admit our need. We can celebrate our grit, but also welcome our groans.

Let's embrace the ways this cultural value empowers us, but let us also reject the ways in which it cuts us off from our bodies, our communities, our children, and our own humanity. Let's model for our children how to live as wholehearted people who aren't afraid to taste all of the flavors life has to offer us.

PART 5

FINDING OUR TRIBE

Tigers are solitary creatures, but when the females are raising their cubs, they often gather together to live in groups.[67] Even tigers know they need mutual support in caring for their young. How much more essential is it for us as humans—who are wired for connection and community[68]—to find our "tribe."[a] We are not meant to live independently, but interdependently. Especially as we seek to sustain lasting change in our homes, our society, and beyond, it's essential for us to find supportive community and to see ourselves as part of a greater whole.

While untigering does require healing from our childhood wounds, shifting our mindset, and rewiring our instincts, growth is not just a matter of choosing to think differently and white-knuckling our way to becoming better parents. We need others to lean on when we feel stuck and weak. We need resources and community so that we are not living in perpetual stress and survival mode. To borrow from recovery language, we need to surrender to a "higher power" and receive the support from others who are on this journey.

We need community where we can find belonging, support, and safety; one that is held together by shared identity, shared values, and shared love, not by fear or fences. When we don't see ourselves clearly, it helps to have others who can point us back to our true selves with compassion. When we are tempted to fall back on our tiger parenting ways, we need those who can show us another way. When we are at the end of our ropes, these people can rally around us and hold us up.

Julianne Holt-Lunstad, professor of psychology at Brigham Young University, has this to say about the necessity of social connections: "Humans need others to survive. Regardless of one's sex, country or culture of origin, or age or economic background, social connection is crucial to human development, health, and survival."[69]

---

a   I use the term "tribe" in a zoological context, not an anthropological one. Although tiger groups are not tribes, I use it here for simplicity's sake.

Bottom line: we need each other.

But how do we find our people in a world that seems so fractured and lonely? Why do we feel so socially impoverished when we're surrounded by more social connectivity than ever?

In this section, we will explore the reasons behind our lack of community and ways we can go about finding it.

CHAPTER 24

RECLAIMING COLLECTIVISM

The collectivism of Asian cultures is often derided and devalued by the individualist Western societies in which many of us grew up. We are shamed for not being assertive enough ("Speak up! The squeaky wheel gets the oil!"), independent enough ("You still live with your parents?!"), unique enough ("All you Asians look the same."). We are stereotyped as timid, group-oriented followers.

In resistance to this stereotype, I myself have often scorned traditional Chinese values like humility, harmony, and interdependence. I have glorified individualism. I prize autonomy, free thinking, and self-actualization—I am American, after all! And yet the deeper I dig, the more I recognize that my beliefs and values have been colonized by individualistic Western thinking.

I believe we are coming to a place in our collective consciousness where we're questioning the individualist approach to parenting and family life. We are siloed in our own worlds and suffering under the weight of carrying this responsibility on our own when the care of children was meant to be a communal endeavor.

How did we get here?

The Whitewashing of Maslow's Hierarchy of Needs

Abraham Maslow is an influential thinker who has helped to shape the Western concept of individualism. Considered by many to be the founder of humanistic psychology, he is most well known for his theory of the hierarchy of needs. He used a triangle framework, with basic needs like food and sleep on the bottom and self-actualization at the top. Many of us have been influenced by Maslow's framework as a foundation of understanding ourselves and our motivations. And yet there are critics that claim his brand of psychology is too individualistic and elitist.[70] It focuses too much on the idea of "self" and self-development without recognizing the need for change on the societal level.

What few of us know is that Maslow actually appropriated his theory from the indigenous Blackfoot nation of Alberta, Canada.[71] After visiting their reserve and observing their way of life, he used what he learned to develop his 1943 paper "A Theory of Human Motivation," where he introduced his hierarchy of needs. Unfortunately, like all things that are culturally appropriated, the essence was lost as Maslow took what was meant to be collective and made it individualistic. The Blackfoot's original conceptualization was a tipi (similar to Maslow's triangular diagram), but instead of self-actualization being at the top, self-actualization actually formed the foundation at the bottom, with community actualization above it and cultural perpetuity at the top.[72]

According to Blackfoot understanding, the development of the individual is meant to just be a starting point for the development of the collective and the endurance of culture, not an end in itself. Needs and motivations are not limited to the scope of the individual or one lifetime, but are considered in the context of the greater sphere of community and with an expansive view of time across generations. It's unfortunate that Maslow replaced this relational, spiritual, and timeless worldview for an individualistic, humanistic, and temporal one.

Thankfully, we are not beholden to these individualistic values. We can find other ways of understanding ourselves and our relationship to those around us. We need not look any further than our own indigenous cultures and other collective societies around us. We need to reclaim this pro-social and interdependent view of ourselves that strengthens our children and families. Instead of seeing our collectivism as something shameful, we must honor and value it. There is so much beauty in considering the "us" and not just the "me."

Social Connections Lead to Greater Well-being

In 2015, Dr. Brett Ford and her colleagues published a study titled "Culture Shapes Whether the Pursuit of Happiness Predicts Higher or Lower Well-Being."[73] Participants from the U.S., Germany, Russia, Japan, and Taiwan were surveyed to see if a high motivation to pursue happiness actually led to more happiness. The results showed that for Americans, a high motivation paradoxically led to lower well-being; for Germans, there was no effect; but for Russians and East Asians, it led to greater well-being.

The difference lies in cultural definitions of happiness.

People who come from individualistic cultures (in this case, Americans and Germans) pursue happiness in ways that generally focus on the self—engaging in a hobby you enjoy, rewarding yourself with a vacation, etc. In contrast, people who come from collectivist cultures pursue happiness in more relational ways—spending time with family and friends, helping others, etc. Since "social connection is one of the most robust predictors of well-being (Helliwell & Putnam, 2004), the pursuit of happiness may yield higher well-being in cultures that promote a socially engaged pursuit of happiness."[74]

In other words, collectivism encourages us to pursue happiness in socially connected ways that benefit not only ourselves, but others. Instead of an antisocial, individualistic definition of happiness that ultimately does not improve our well-being, our collectivism and pursuit of connection actually make us happier. Understanding this can help us to prioritize community care rather than simply focusing on our own needs. Much of what we define as "self-care" falls under individualistic pursuits, yet sadly fails to increase our joy. In fact, it can actually impair it. The way self-care is marketed to us is often about retreating from others and treating ourselves—relying on ourselves and tending to our own needs. Yet these can also be the very things that prevent us from getting the support that we require. While we can take steps to develop healthy boundaries and self-love as parents, we also must resist the lie that we have to be self-sufficient in meeting all the needs of our family.

Social Connections Improve Our Health

Healthy social connections are necessary for our human flourishing. Without a supportive network of relationships with family, friends, and others in our community, we are not only less happy, but more at risk for addiction,[75] depression,[76] disease,[77] and even death. The inverse is true as well: having strong connections contributes to our mental and physical health. Positive social interactions help increase the dopamine, oxytocin, and endorphins we produce,[78] creating positive physiological responses in our brains and bodies.

One study with rats showed that social connections had a pronounced impact on substance abuse addiction.[79] When given a choice, the rats repeatedly showed a preference for social interaction over drugs. Even rats who were compulsively self-administering drugs for multiple weeks prior immediately stopped or decreased their drug use when placed in an environment where there was social interaction with other rats. Furthermore, social interaction prevented the escalation of drug-seeking behavior. It actually changed the neurobiology of the rats, inhibiting their drug cravings.

While health issues are obviously complex and multi-layered, helping our kids to foster healthy connections will go a long way in helping them to be resilient, robust, and resistant to harmful influences. Whether for ourselves or our children, we all need meaningful, caring relationships with others in order to flourish in mind, body, and spirit.

Prioritizing Social Connections over External Gains

In the 2018 Happiness Report,[80] Latin Americans reported high levels of happiness despite socio-political and economic factors that would suggest otherwise (high corruption, high crime rates, high poverty, etc.). The reason? Positive and warm family and social relationships. Social capital was more predictive of happiness than financial or political capital.

I think there's a lesson to be learned here. The research shows us that if we have strong relationships, we can experience a sense of well-being even with limited economic and political power. The inverse is not true, however. The United States prides itself on its democratic freedoms and high GDP but ranks among the highest in rates of mental health or substance use disorders in the world.[81]

In our personal pursuit of happiness, we often invest more time and energy on gaining power and wealth than on nurturing our interpersonal relationships. In our collective pursuit of economic, political, and social justice, we sometimes overemphasize the outward markers of happiness defined by individualistic and capitalistic systems: high salaries, expensive cars, the number of degrees we've earned. We have bought into the values of power, wealth, and status, fighting for our access to them instead of recognizing how they can often undermine our relationships. Long hours at work, running the rat race, the focus on materialism and external gains—our lives and even our activism have been colonized. Even traditionally collectivist cultures like China are becoming increasingly disconnected and individualistic because of dramatic economic development.[82]

For many of us who are in the midst of destabilizing economic and political climates, our relational connections are more important than ever. We need to be intentional about prioritizing personal relationships despite societal demands and pressures. It's time to realign our lifestyle and return to our collective and connected values so that decisions about our family culture, our work, our schedules, our spending, and our votes reflect those values.

Collectivism Can Inform our Fight for Social Justice

While collectivism can promote a strong sense of family and community, group-oriented cultures also obviously have their own pathologies—authoritarian tactics used to keep everyone in line, pressure to conform to social expectations, unhealthy enmeshment, lack of boundaries, the disregard of individual autonomy for the sake of the "greater good." All these are hindrances to creating healthy families, social connections, and social change.

Furthermore, it can also reinforce lines of who is in and who is out. It can be notoriously difficult for outsiders to build meaning-ful relationships in such societies. In Japan, social relationships are defined by those considered uchi (inside group) and those considered soto (outside group)[83]; in China there is the aforementioned concept of 关系 guanxi (the system of social networks and relationships a person has). In such cultures, people are often willing to sacrifice for the good of those within their own circles but feel little incentive to care for those outside those tight relationships. This has played out in what is known as "China's bystander problem"[84] where passersby on the street heartlessly ignore a strangers' distress and refuse to help, often leading to tragic deaths that could have easily been avoided.

Still, I believe there is much about collectivism that can be reclaimed and redeemed. By redefining and expanding the bound-aries of who we include in our in-group, we can have a framework of community care that fuels and sustains our fight for social justice. A collectivist view can motivate us to consider not only what is best for ourselves and our people, but what is best for the whole. It can move us to willingly lay down our privileges and sacrifice for the greater good. It can inspire us to work together for change, shar-ing our resources instead of competing with one another. We don't need to step on the backs of others, climbing the socio-economic ladder and improving our personal lives at the expense of other mar-ginalized communities. Especially in diverse societies like America, where ethnic communities tend to only consider how policies and laws affect them and theirs, we need to widen our circles and work towards a vision of "us" that extends beyond our own network and cares for our neighbor as ourselves.

While top-down, systemic change is necessary to create more peace and prosperity for society as a whole, our activism needs to be a grassroots movement from the bottom up, focused on supporting families and communities. Like the Blackfoot, we need to think of justice and development within a communal rather than individual framework. Creating a more conducive environment for happiness to flourish is needed—more just policies, increased financial stability, and greater access to social services are important factors to our well-being. But those institutional shifts need to stem from a place of relational connection and a desire for mutual prosperity.

———————◆———————

The beauty of the Blackfoot worldview is that it doesn't pit individualism against collectivism but sees self-actualization as fundamental for collective well-being. Individuals who have strong social connections—but also the freedom to live out their true selves—will ultimately benefit the group. Individualism and collectivism don't have to be on opposite sides of the spectrum; we can find creative ways that seek to honor the personal and the political, the private and the public.

When we see parenting within this framework, we can approach our family life and the caring of our children in ways that are wholistic and communal, rooted in respect and relationship.

CHAPTER 25

IT TAKES A VILLAGE

W
e often throw around the phrase, "It takes a village to raise a child," when talking about parenting. It's used to describe the need for a network of people to support the healthy development of a child. However, this concept should not be relegated to the realm of child-rearing. All human flourishing requires interconnectedness, and yet, sadly, our society is not structured in a way that fosters this kind of village.

In traditional Chinese culture, society was formed around multi-generational communities consisting of grandparents, aunties, uncles, cousins, friends, and neighbors. We can see this is in many aspects of our culture, like the way we eat (family-style around a big round table); the precise nomenclature for each family member (different titles for each and every relative depending on exactly how you're related); the involvement of extended family in the caring of children. Even the 四合院, the court-yard houses of ancient China, were designed to accommodate an extended family and provide an enclosed space that encouraged communal living and family orientation.[85] Embedded throughout traditional Chinese culture is this understanding and celebration of "village."

Unfortunately, the modern lifestyle in both the East and West is quickly losing this sense of community. Few of us have tight-knit networks where we and our children feel known and cared for—someone we can call on at the drop of a hat in our time of need, someone that we do life with. Parents and children alike are so over-scheduled and busy that we don't have time to build trust and friendship with our neighbors. We're all so caught up in the hustle that we can barely offer each other the one thing that is needful—our presence. Even in this age of unlimited social connectivity, many of us still feel lonely and lacking support.

I've experienced this village-less-ness, but I've also experienced glimpses of village throughout my years as a parent—the homeschool co-op in China that we were a part of for six years; kids in the neighborhood who would drop in to play unannounced; beloved aunties and uncles who loved our kids; dear friends who walked with us through births, deaths, and all the everyday moments in between.

As I am transitioning back to life in the States after many years abroad, this idea of "village" has been on my mind. How can I be intentional about fostering community for myself and my family? How can I help build this village that we all so desperately need? We can't all travel back in time or move out to an actual village. What does it look like to start changing our cultural values in this modern world that we live in?

Obviously, I don't have all the answers. There are many systemic forces that work against this formation of meaningful community. All I know is that I can bemoan my lack of village, resenting and resigning myself to the fact that close friendships haven't magically fallen into my lap; or I can try to resist these forces and my own jadedness for the sake of my family and the collective society. I know the latter is the only option.

Here are some radical acts of counter-cultural living that can help build our sense of village.

Align with Your Values

Although all of us are affected by the cultural forces around us, there's still much that we can do to define our own family culture and begin reshaping society around us. Firstly, we can become aware of the steady diet of "junk values"[86] that is being force-fed to us and our children—those that focus on image, materialism, power, and prestige. We can expose it for what it is, like actress Jameela Jamil[87] who is speaking out against body shaming, diet culture, and misogyny. These junk values that are perpetuated in culture do not help us to foster our true selves or true community. They serve as smoke and mirrors to distract us from the hard work of vulnerability, authenticity, and intimacy.

We can consciously choose a different path and go against the cultural current. In a world that values being independent, we can value connection. In a world that values strength and power, we can value vulnerability and humility. In a world that values productivity, we can value rest and play.

Take some time and assess what is really important to you and your family. Write down at least 5 values that you want defining your life. Then, take steps to start aligning your lifestyle so it reflects those values.

When we live in alignment with our values, there will be others with similar values who naturally come alongside us. We will fall in step with others who are on a similar path and headed to a similar destination. I have found this to be true in my own life, whether it's been in regards to my progressive faith, peaceful parenting, or unschooling. When I had the courage to live in resonance with my beliefs, I found a village of people who resonated as well.

Slow Down

As I write this chapter, the world is currently dealing with the coronavirus pandemic and most of us have been forced to slow down. While it has been disruptive, to say the least, it's also been an opportunity to reevaluate our pace of life and consider how we can live more sustainably and mindfully as we move forward. The modern lifestyle is so fast-paced and driven that it prevents us from fostering that community that we need to thrive. It doesn't naturally allow for families to share life together unless one makes a concerted effort. Hours away at school/work and busy schedules make it difficult for us to connect with those within our family, let alone those outside our family. It's a very mechanical way of existing: standardization, compartmentalization, productivity. Go, go, go, go—24/7, 365 days a year.

This is not how our bodies, souls, and relationships are designed to function and grow. We aren't meant to be machines that are constantly running. The natural flow of life and nature is much more agrarian than industrial. There is day and night, rest and activity, springtime and harvest, life and death. We have rhythms and seasons. Slowing down so that we can go with the flow frees us to be intuitive and intentional about ourselves and our relationships. It gives us the time and opportunity to build trust and friendship with one another. It builds in margin so that we have the capacity to be available for each other, love each other deeply, and serve each other well.

That's not to say that this comes without a cost. Oftentimes, slowing down means we become less valuable to the capitalistic industrial complex. It may mean we earn less money, can't afford to eat out all the time, and forgo the house in the gated community. When we were living in China, Jason purposely chose a teaching job at a university that had stability and a flexible schedule, even though the salary wasn't great. When we moved back to the States, he didn't return to his previous career as an engineer but decided instead on a 9 to 5 administrative job. The freedom to spend more time with the family and pursue his interests were more valuable than a large income.

Likewise, we may lose social capital for not keeping up with the latest trends, cool activities, or demanding practice schedules. We may choose to have our child join the local sports league instead of the traveling team, or sign them up for only one summer camp instead of scheduling a coding course, sleepaway camp, and hip hop classes at the community center back-to-back.

Maybe because I'm naturally a low-energy introvert, this appeals to me. Others who have more capacity or enjoy more activity may chafe at the suggestion to slow down. My point is not to suggest that we eliminate all busyness or return to the bucolic days of the past. Every family needs to find their own sweet spot that best supports them in creating the life and community they desire. The point is to mindfully choose a lifestyle that serves us instead of enslaves us. We don't have to jump on the hamster wheel or run the rat race just because everyone else is! There can be a better way if we have the courage to choose it.

Be Vulnerable

Being vulnerable means that we risk showing our true selves to others—one that is not polished or perfect. This is the only way that we can experience true community. True intimacy and community are formed when we are accepted as we truly are, but we must allow ourselves to be seen and known in order for that to happen. Not just the curated or filtered version of ourselves, but all the messy parts that make us feel exposed too. If we don't show up in spaces as our authentic selves, any connections we make are counterfeit because they were made with our false persona. We end up feeling even lonelier, unable to experience intimacy and "known-ness" because we haven't shown up as our true selves.

I discovered this myself one day when a friend described me as 温柔 (literally "gentle and soft"), praising me for being a tender mother, gracious host, and good cook—pretty much the epitome of a good housewife. It was meant to be a compliment, yet I had a visceral reaction against it. It left me feeling unknown and misunderstood. As I reflected on why, I realized that this person was seeing a projection of myself while missing my essence. All the parts of me that I value most—my intensity, my feistiness, my intellect, my ideas, my ideals—had been erased. Although I felt hurt, I didn't fault my friend. I realized that I wasn't showing up authentically. I was playing a part. I was performing in order to meet people's expectations. If I wanted people to see me as ME, I needed to be willing to offer my whole self.

This feeling of being understood and appreciated doesn't usually happen quickly or easily, however. Intimate relationships are usually built little by little, moment by moment; we have to be willing to put in the time and effort to develop that trust. We can begin by putting out bids for deeper connection, small investments of honesty and realness. This can feel scary and risky, but I believe the world is truly starving for this kind of vulnerability. When we have the courage to take the first step toward authenticity, there will be those who will be drawn to it and respond in kind.

That's not to say that everyone is worthy of our vulnerability, unfortunately. There are people and spaces that are unsafe, villages where a cozy bonfire can quickly turn into a burning stake. We've seen it happen to others. Perhaps we've been burned ourselves. These people are not our village. We do not offer our true selves recklessly to those who would not treasure it. Sharing our deepest, darkest secrets right off the bat may fast track us to intimacy yet leave us susceptible to betrayal because the other person has not proven their trustworthiness. No, our vulnerability is a gift we offer to those who have earned our trust.

Practice Hospitality

Hospitality is something that doesn't come naturally to some of us (or is it just me?), especially when we've been conditioned to have a scarcity mindset. We can barely manage our own family's needs, let alone think about caring for others. Opening up our lives, homes, and hearts to others can feel like a drain on our energy, time, resources, and emotions.

But we don't have to see it that way. We can reframe hospitality as something that benefits everyone involved. Serving others, whether it's inside or outside our home, gets us out of our survivalist mentality that focuses on scarcity and self. It helps to create an environment when we expand the borders of our heart and invites us to look up from our navel-gazing. It may take practice and effort to overcome the inertia, but it will ultimately make us happier and more connected.

My brother-in-law and his wife are networkers and gatherers. They host block parties and invite all the neighbors, serving up homemade popcorn and cotton candy, passing out balloon animals, and busting out the karaoke machine with flashing disco lights. Their hospitality and openness have contributed to creating a neighborhood that really watches out for each other and trusts each other. Even when they recently moved to a new city, they didn't wait around for neighbors to welcome them. They were proactive and took the first step in getting to know people in their community. It didn't take long before they were once again busting out the popcorn and karaoke machine.

Hospitality doesn't need to look like a big block party or hosting a bunch of people in your home, however. Not all of us have the energy or desire to connect with people that way. We can focus on one-on-one relationships or smaller groups. We can take the pressure off and host a potluck or "crappy dinner party"[88] where you make whatever you have in the fridge and focus on the guests instead of on impressing them. Hospitality should never feel like an obligation or competition, but something that is an authentic expression of our care for others.

Receive Help

Receiving help and hospitality are just different sides of the same coin. There is giving when we are able, but there is also receiving. In this culture where neediness is frowned upon, it takes courage to admit that we don't have it all together; that we need others. This challenges the unhealthy elevation of self-sufficiency, independence, and the assumption of able-bodiedness. Asking for what we need creates an environment of mutuality and interdependence where we look out for each other and serve one another.

This requires us to change our mindset about receiving help. If we see our own needs as a weakness or a burden on others, we will also view others in the same way when they share their needs. We will judge them, lack compassion, and expect them to pull themselves up by their bootstraps. But when we can show ourselves compassion and be honest with our vulnerabilities, we are more able to extend that same grace to others. It can be a lesson in humility to admit that we need help, but we can see it as an opportunity to share our humanity and foster mutual care.

We don't need to wait until we're in desperate straits before we ask for help. It can start off small, like asking a neighbor to accept a package for you, or calling a friend for parenting advice. Doing so lets other people know that they can also call us up and lean on us when it's their turn to be in a bind. Far from being a dead weight, we actually can add value by helping build a community that looks out for one another instead of one where we all suffer alone in silence.

Do Life Together

Instead of seeing our family as an isolated unit, trying to stay afloat by doing everything on our own, we can realize that other families are also looking for support. Many hands make light work when we band together and share resources. We can gather together with other families for batch-cooking nights or do regular meal swaps. We can have playgroups together with other parents. We can participate in carpools or homeschool collectives—anything where the burden of responsibility is shared and we know we're not alone.

I have personally experienced the benefit of having friends nearby with whom I could do life together. As much as I love and appreciate my online communities, I also know the necessity of having friends in the flesh nearby who are there for the unexceptional, everyday moments of life as well as the crises; having people who can hold my baby, give me a hug, invite me over for dinner, or help watch my kids at the drop of a hat.

But it's not just building personal friendships; getting to know people in the community also creates a strong sense of village. When we lived in China, we'd chat with the lady in our apartment complex who guarded our bikes; we knew the delivery guy who came to our door almost every day to drop off packages; we always went to the same hairdresser who would cut our kids' hair for 15 yuan; we bought 烧饼 (Chinese flatbread) from the same family at our market; we'd salute the old 爷爷 (elderly man) as we passed him on our evening walks. Seeing these neighborhood people day in and day out helped us feel connected to them and the community.

Not all of us may be ready to move into a commune, but intentionality is needed to create counter-cultural communities. Make it a point to get to know your neighbors, choose to live near close friends, or even consider shared housing. Redefine family lines to include those who may be more isolated—single mothers, refugee families, individuals living on their own. Widening our circles expands our hearts and strengthens our communities.

Share Resources

When I first began raising my kids in China, good-quality toys, clothes, books, and household items were difficult to find. We couldn't go down to the local mall or shop online to find what we needed, so we created a culture of sharing instead. There was always a steady supply of hand-me-down clothes and other resources being passed from one family to another; I even remember a coveted toy slide brought over from America that made its way through at least 5 different families. We fostered a gift economy and practiced "reciprocal altruism"[89] where we gave to each other freely without expecting compensation.

When I moved back to the States, I didn't think that I would find a similar community until I stumbled upon my local Buy Nothing group. These groups are hyper-local gift economies that offer people a way to give and receive, share, lend, borrow, and express gratitude. Some of the principles that drive the Buy Nothing project are listed below:

- We believe our hyper-local groups strengthen the social fabric of their communities and ensure the health and vitality of each member.

- We come from a place of abundance ~ not scarcity.
- We do not buy, sell, trade, barter, or otherwise exchange money for items or services.
- We measure wealth by the personal connections made and trust between people.
- We value people and their stories and narratives above the "stuff."
- We are inclusive at our core.
- We believe every community has the same wealth of generosity and abundance.[90]

Through my Buy Nothing group, I have received homegrown vegetables, fruit and herbs, baked goods, jewelry, household items, and even a beautiful Chinese antique cabinet. The generosity of others inspires me to be generous as well, and I have found just as much pleasure in giving as I have in receiving. I have loved the spirit of generosity and gratitude that is cultivated through this gift economy. Check out www.buynothingproject.org for more details, or start something similar in your own neighborhood!

Sharing resources with our neighbors and friends creates tighter communities as we connect with each other and look out for each other. While it strengthens our local neighborhoods, it also benefits our global village by helping us to reduce and rethink our consumption and environmental impact. Instead of mindlessly buying, hoarding, and disposing, this culture of giving teaches us to take and use only what we need and share the rest.

Lean on Family

Our collectivist view of family can be a healthier alternative to the framework of single-family households that often leaves parents burnt out and frazzled. We have the intergenerational relationships that include grandparents and extended family, but also a whole network of 叔叔们 (uncles) and 阿姨们 (aunties) who aren't related to us but still care for us. In China, it is assumed that grandparents will help take care of children while the parents work. Among many Asian families, intergenerational households are common and interdependence is celebrated. In contrast, the Western ideals of self-sufficiency and being "self-made" often cause outsiders to look condescendingly on these values and family systems.

I remember being at the wedding rehearsal dinner of my Korean American friend. His white groomsman was mocking him because the father of the groom was the one footing the bill for the expensive wedding. The groomsman saw this as a source of shame, believing that a grown man in his late 30s should pay for his own wedding. I bristled when I heard his comment. Such a view is a very colonized way of thinking about money, resources, and family; it does not reflect the reality of many indigenous and collectivist cultures that share intergenerational wealth. As an Asian American, I don't have to internalize these ideals of self-reliance and independence that ignore our human need for community and interdependence. I can see my family's collective values as a privilege instead of a disgrace—grandparents who are willing to regularly watch our kids, parents who will help pay for tuition or a down payment on a house—we can be thankful for the ways that our cultural heritage has a built-in "village" where extended family and different generations care for the needs of the group.

When my sons were born, my mother offered to fly out to China to stay with me for a month. At first, I was a little concerned about having my mom live with us for such a long time, but when I came home from the hospital with a newborn in my arms and no idea how to take care of him, I was grateful for her presence. She cooked me ginger pig's feet and fish soup to encourage my body to heal and my milk to come in. She held and rocked my baby to sleep so I could rest. She fussed over how I violated every rule of 坐月子, the Chinese tradition of one month postpartum confinement. My mother's help was a gift to me, especially as many new parents lack this type of support and mothers are expected to bounce back quickly after giving birth.

Granted, there are unhealthy ways that our families get involved in our lives when we'd rather they not. Healthy boundaries are necessary so that interdependence doesn't devolve into co-dependence. This can be especially difficult in many Asian family systems, but instead of perpetuating toxic cultural and familial patterns, we can choose to be the generation that breaks the cycle and starts a new pattern. Sadly, for some of us that means *not* including certain family members in our "village." We may have to look outside our biological family to find a chosen family that can help provide that support system we need. Either way, it's good to acknowledge our need to intentionally create connections; to celebrate our desire for community instead of putting on an armor of self-sufficiency.

Be Aware of Your Capacity and Personality

There are those like my friend Sylvia who always have people in their homes and appointments on their calendars. She is a community organizer, a public servant, a board member of non-profits, a pastor's wife, and a busy mom. Such people are high-energy extroverts who feel enlivened by frequent interactions. Then there are those like me who secretly rejoice when a social engagement gets canceled and avert their eyes when asked to volunteer. Not all of us have the same capacity, resources, energy, or personality to constantly be putting ourselves out there. Instead of a one-size-fits-all approach to building our village, it's important to do it in a way that is sustainable and authentic to us.

Some of us may be facing challenges like chronic pain, mental illness, or other special needs. Some of us may be in a season of grieving, intense focus on a project, or mindful solitude. Some of us just have a lower tolerance for noise, activity, and busyness. We may need to get out of our comfort zones and push past our fears, but we also need to be gentle and compassionate with ourselves. Each of us should give as freely as we are able without comparison to others. And if we're unable to give for the time being, there's still plenty we can do: align with our values, slow down, be vulnerable, ask for help, do it together, lean on family... all of these still help lay the groundwork for the community we need as we raise up the next generation together.

CHAPTER 26

PEACEFUL PARENTING IS COMMUNAL

While building a village is vital for thriving families, peaceful parenting goes beyond simply building strong connections and finding supportive community. It is a communal endeavor. It expands outside the four walls of our homes and past the streets of our neighborhoods to the greater social context we live in. It requires us to zoom out beyond a molecular view of the nuclear family and view parenting through both a micro and a macro lens—understanding triggers, brain science, and emotional intelligence, **as well as** recognizing how intersectional social factors and systems influence parenting.

If we are serious about challenging and changing the cultural norms around parenting, we must consider how to dismantle systemic oppression that creates undue stress on children, parents, and families.

Understand Our Privilege

If you think it's hard to not lash out at your kids when you have a partner, a steady income, a membership at the yoga studio, and a house cleaner who comes every Wednesday, imagine how hard it must be for someone who doesn't have those same means or support.

Imagine parenting as a single mom, an immigrant, or as a person who fears for their life because of their race, faith, or sexual orientation. Consider what it might be like to live in an authoritarian and patriarchal culture that finds peaceful parenting completely foreign, rather than in a country that upholds democratic ideals and celebrates individual autonomy.

I recognize the many privileges I have as a parent: a committed partner who is a loving and engaged father, physically and mentally healthy family members, a stable income with a flexible schedule that allows me to stay home, and easy access to peaceful parenting resources in English.

But just as I understand my privilege, I understand my lack of it as well. Many peaceful parenting resources feel inaccessible to me because they do not take my cultural background into consideration—the cultural codes, perspectives, and expectations that make emotional connection and respect for my children challenging. Few of us Asian Americans have experienced peaceful parenting in our own lives, and lack culturally relevant role models to emulate. That is what motivated me to start the Untigering blog and the Untigering Parents[91] group: to address the unique obstacles that many members of the Asian diaspora face on the road toward peaceful parenting.

This twofold understanding of privilege keeps us humble as we recognize both the benefits we enjoy and the burdens we carry into our parenting. Acknowledging our own privilege gives us compassion for others. Acknowledging our lack of privilege gives us compassion for ourselves.

Recognize How Social Issues Affect Parenting

However much we'd like to believe that we can protect our children from outside forces, social, political, and economic issues inevitably affect our family dynamics. Rather than judging other parents for struggling, we have to be aware of these pressures and stresses so that we can show compassion and stand in solidarity with them against oppression.

Let's take racism, for example. In 2018, U.S. child abuse rates[92] by race of the victim showed Native Americans with the highest percentage and African Americans following closely behind. Asian Americans came in lowest. It would be pretty easy to make gross generalizations about certain racial groups based on this data, but doing so would completely ignore how racism contributes to family trauma.

Ta-Nehisi Coates, in his brutal memoir *Between the World and Me*, wrote of how many Black parents resort to violence against their children in an attempt to protect them from violence from the police. "Now I personally understood my father and the old mantra—'Either I can beat him or the police.' I understood it all—the cable wires, the extension cords, the ritual switch. Black people love their children with a kind of obsession. You are all we have, and you come to us endangered."[93]

In Sherman Alexie's novel, *The Absolutely True Diary of a Part-Time Indian*[94] Junior's father is an alcoholic, disappearing for days and weeks at a time. Rowdy's father beats him. But the withdrawal, addiction, rage, and violence that we see played out in the foreground have a backdrop of Native American subjugation. "We Indians have lost everything. We lost our native land, we lost our languages, we lost our songs and dances. We lost each other. We only know how to lose and be lost."

Racially oppressed communities face systemic obstacles that make it difficult for them to gain wealth, receive support, have access to education and resources, and fully embrace their cultural and ethnic identities. Such social stressors inevitably affect one's ability to parent with empathy, mindfulness, and respect. Calmly navigating down the road of parenting is challenging in the best of times, but how can people be expected to do so when their engine is bad, gas is low, tire is flat, and air conditioning is out, all while hauling a heavy trailer in the back?

Although abusive parenting should rightly be denounced, parents of such communities are also the ones most often punished and criminalized for such behavior. Racial profiling distorts the reporting of child neglect and abuse, making certain groups more vulnerable to the scrutiny and intervention of government authorities while other groups are given a pass. Whether it's the welfare queen, alcoholic deadbeat, or model minority, such stereotypes perpetuate a vicious cycle that only serves to confirm biases about who makes good parents and who doesn't.

Racism is just one issue—imagine those living in war-torn communities, under totalitarian governments, or without access to basic necessities. Instead of berating those who are struggling, let's recognize the host of social issues that parents (ourselves included) may be dealing with, whether racism, classism, sexism, ableism, or the many other ways we humans use power over one another.

Let's withhold judgment, resist the labels, and seek to understand each other's stories while doing the work to fight against systems of oppression.

Support Marginalized Communities

Understanding how social issues affect our parenting encourages us to work towards a more equitable society where all families can thrive. Our advocacy for peaceful parenting must be paired with advocacy for marginalized communities. We must ask ourselves how we can support families that are most at risk because of lack of power, education, resources, and wealth.

When I lived in China, I was involved in work with orphanages and sexually exploited women. Most children in orphanages are not truly orphans but have been abandoned because of poverty, disabilities, favoring of boys, lack of support for unwed mothers, etc. Poor women from less developed areas are often compelled to leave their children and become sex workers for similar reasons. Instead of faulting struggling parents for the desperate measures they take, we can work on community development and prevention, providing support and resources so that families can stay intact. We can educate and speak out against beliefs that devalue children, women, and those with special needs.

Wherever we live, we can find ways to assist marginalized groups through:

- our amplification of their voices
- our advocacy
- our protest
- our vote
- our volunteer work
- our financial support.

Affirming the dignity of our children necessitates that we affirm the dignity of all human beings. If we truly care about the welfare of children, we must be engaged in addressing the greater social ills that hinder the formation of healthy families. We must work together against oppression and on behalf of social justice so that we reap the collective benefits that will help us all to thrive as a community.

PART 6

FINAL THOUGHTS

CHAPTER 27

CULTURE SHAPERS AND CHANGE MAKERS

I recently did a search on Instagram for #asianparenting, looking for resources to share on social media. The results were disappointing. Most of the posts reinforced the stereotype of the typical Chinese tiger parent: domineering, demanding, and difficult to please.

I don't know about you, but I'm tired of that trope. I'm ready to start changing the narrative that "Chinese parenting" equals tiger parenting. I'm ready to start shifting the cultural norms so that abuse and oppression of children are no longer acceptable.

"I Contain Multitudes"

Culture is made and remade by people like you and me. It is not something solid or steadfast across time. It is something constantly in flux and open to suggestion. Instead of assuming that we are powerless against cultural norms, we need to understand that we have the ability to resist, act upon, and alter culture. Part of that work involves us acknowledging our own complex and intersectional identities that do not conform to the limits of any one culture.

Growing up, I loved telling others the interesting fact that each of my family members was born in a different country. My dad was born in China, my mom in Vietnam, my older sister in Hong Kong (which was a British colony at the time), I in the U.S., and my younger brother in Canada. My parents always joked that if they had had another kid, they would have flown out to Australia to give birth.

Even though I was born in the States, the reality is that my heart, my values, and my culture are connected to other parts of the world. I grew up in Edmonton, Alberta, and it was there that I discovered hockey legend Wayne Gretzky, first tasted delicious Ukrainian perogies, began studying French, and learned how to survive -20°C winters. Throughout my childhood, I made regular visits to Hong Kong to "get in touch with my roots." There, I fell in love with Cantonese culture and experienced my first taste of independence—navigating the MTR and sipping on Vitasoy Lemon Teas while shopping at 女人街 (Ladies' Market). My high school years were spent in small town Americana where cow-tipping was considered a teenage pastime. Despite being the only Chinese American in my class, I was proud of my roots, serving as president of the Asian American club and wearing a cheongsam to my senior prom long before it became popular for white girls to do so.

In contrast, the large college I attended had an undergraduate population that was nearly 40% Asian[95] and was located in one of the most socially liberal cities in the United States. I majored in English with an emphasis on Victorian literature, but my interests were not exclusively Anglophilic—I was also just a few credits shy of minoring in Asian studies. I graduated, got married, and a few years later moved to Northeast China where I picked up Mandarin Chinese, started a family, and raised my kids in a city of 16 million people. I lived in that city longer than I have lived anywhere.

I share all this because it shows how I don't belong to just one place, one culture. I am not confined by any one set of norms and rules. Instead, I hold in my body a vast array of influences, values, experiences, sounds, smells, tastes, and ways of seeing. As Walt Whitman puts it,

"I am large, I contain multitudes."[96]

I am rich in my complexities and paradoxes as a multicultural person. In China, I may not be Chinese enough, and in America, I may not be American enough, but my goal is not to fit into those strict, well-marked boxes. It's to be unapologetically and wholly myself so that I can expand the borders of what it means to be a Chinese American woman and mother.

Likewise, our societies and cultures contain multitudes, often in contradiction to each other. Culture is something that is dynamic rather than static, manifold rather than uniform, porous rather than pure. Yet the radical nationalism and ethnic tribalism echoing around the world today ignore this reality. We all belong to each other. We cannot be pinned down to "one nation, under God."

Being global citizens and multicultural people rather than ones who simply pledge their allegiance to one country, one system, and one culture means that we can have a sense of belonging without being *owned*. We develop a synergetic relationship with culture instead of one that is enslaved to it, recognizing our power to shape culture, even as it shapes us.

This empowers us to celebrate **and** challenge the cultures that define us. We can honor the beauty in our indigenous ways of being as well as own up to the unhealthy patterns that we see in our culture. We can appreciate the freedoms and privileges we have while honestly calling out broken systems and rejecting internalized white supremacy. We can expose cycles of trauma present in our own cultures: shame, fear, violence, scarcity, racism, authoritarianism, patriarchy, misogyny, abuse. We can be agents of change instead of victims to tradition.

Forget the Tiger. Be Like the Gray Wolf.

In 1995, eight gray wolves were reintroduced to Yellowstone National Park. For 70 years, wolves had been absent from the park and the elk population had gotten out of control. Plant life was being destroyed because of overgrazing and soil erosion was occurring because of the lack of vegetation. The ecosystem of the park was out of balance. Wildlife biologists in Yellowstone wondered if the eradication of wolves had triggered this trophic cascade of ecological changes and decided to bring wolves back into the park's ecosystem. The results were dramatic.

Not only did the wolves hunt and reduce the population of elk, they changed the behavior of the elk. The elk avoided grazing too long in one place or withdrew altogether from areas that left them exposed, allowing willows, aspen, and cottonwood trees to make a comeback. Birds and beavers returned to the area since there were now trees to live in, feed on, and build dams with. The beaver dams created river habitats that were conducive to other animals like otter, ducks, and reptiles. Even the rivers began to change as the regenerating vegetation reduced soil erosion and strengthened the riverbanks. The reintroduction of the wolves led to all these chains of events, the effects of which are still rippling out and being discovered to this day.[97]

We, likewise, have the potential to influence our environment. We are not bound to the current parenting norms of our culture or society. We can be like the wolves in Yellowstone, transforming ourselves, our families, and our communities for future generations through the choices that we make today. We can bring healing, life, and flourishing to the world around us through our untigering.

If you come from a cultural heritage that is steeped in the oppression of children, just know that culture is made and remade by people like you and me. Let's be brave and bold as we challenge the conventional wisdom and status quo of parenting. Like those gray wolves, let's be change makers and cycle breakers who alter the trajectory of generations and cultures yet to come.

EPILOGUE

Noah is now 12 and Caleb is 10 as I finish the writing of this book. The other day, we all jumped into our queen-sized bed for a family snuggle, dog piling on top of each other and reveling in our closeness. We've come a long way. We now have peace in our home. The despair that I felt not so long ago as a parent has been replaced by joy and delight. I'm so grateful.

I never imagined I'd be an untigering mother, yet here I am. All along, it was in my blood; all along, it was in my culture. I'm returning to the truest parts of me that are rooted in love and justice. I'm learning to honor my relational and collective values as well as my need for boundaries and autonomy. I'm hopeful that my children and the generations after them will do the same.

And I'm hopeful that the same can be true of you and your family. Even though this is the end of the book, it's really just the beginning of our journey.

Take my hand. Let's continue untigering together.

ENDNOTES

1   https://www.raisingfreepeople.com/
2   Chua, A. (2011). *Battle Hymn of the Tiger Mother.* Penguin Books.
3   Now obviously, this is a caricature of Chinese parenting. In a country of over 1.3 billion people (not including the Chinese diaspora all over the world), there is no ONE way of parenting. Yet I find it helpful to claim the label of tiger parenting for those of us who see our experiences reflected in it.
4   https://www.parentingforbrain.com/4-baumrind-parenting-styles/
5   https://www.urbandictionary.com/define.php?term=parachute%20kids
6   Baumrind, D. (1966). Effects of authoritative parental control on child behavior. *Child Development, 37*(4), 891.
7   https://dictionary.cambridge.org/us/dictionary/english/give-and-take
8   https://www.cdc.gov/violenceprevention/acestudy/fastfact.html
9   https://konmari.com/
10 Nouwen, H. (2017). *Who are we? Henri Nouwen on our Christian identity.* Now You Know Media Inc.
11 Brown, B. (2015). Rising strong. Spiegel & Grau, an imprint of Random House.
12 Gilbert, E. (2016). Big magic: Creative living beyond fear [Kindle version]. Retrieved from http://www.amazon.com/
13 Barrett, L.F. (2017). How emotions are made: The secret life of the brain [Kindle version]. Retrieved from http://www.amazon.com/

14 Barrett, L.F. (2017, December). You aren't at the mercy of your emotions—your brain creates them. [Video file] Retrieved from https://www.ted.com/talks/lisa_feldman_barrett_you_aren_t_at_the_mercy_of_your_emotions_your_brain_creates_them?language=en#t-358034

15 Brett, T. G. (2017, August 20). A new vision of children and childhood. Retrieved from https://parentingforsocialchange.com/a-new-vision-of-children/

16 Tsabary, Shefali. (2010). The conscious parent [Kindle version]. Retrieved from http://www.overdrive.com/

17 http://www.lifelearningmagazine.com/quotes-about-unschooling-life-learning.htm

18 Gordon, T. (n.d.) Children don't misbehave. Retrieved from https://www.gordontraining.com/free-parenting-articles/children-dont-misbehave/

19 https://www.positivediscipline.com/sites/default/files/what-is-positive-discipline.pdf

20 http://childtrauma.org/

21 http://childtrauma.org/

22 Children of more caring, less controlling parents live happier lives. (2018, November 15). UCL News. Retrieved from www.ucl.ac.uk/news/2015/sep/children-more-caring-less-controlling-parents-live-happier-lives.

23 Siegel, D. & Bryson, T. P. (2011). The whole-brain child: 12 revolutionary strategies to nurture your child's developing mind [Kindle Edition]. Retrieved from amazon.com

24 Kennedy-Moore, E. (2018, June 29). What to say to empathize better with your child. Psychology Today. Retrieved from https://www.psychologytoday.com/us/blog/growing-friendships/201806/what-say-empathize-better-your-child?fbclid=IwAR0_ABBAevYhN-pHWi-p8MchBaYPOl-wumUCsVDbgblCEbI3K81FfLO7uLyU

25 https://www.newsweek.com/stronger-steel-85533

26 Fu, P. (2014). Bend, not break. Penguin Books.

27 https://en.wikipedia.org/wiki/Yes,_and...

28 http://reflectionsonwalt.blogspot.com/2018/04/buzz-price-and-power-of-yes-if.html

29 Chua, A. (2011). Battle hymn of the tiger mother (Reprint ed.). Penguin Books. (p. 29)

30 Panne, V. (2020, Jul 6). Is unschooling the way to decolonize education? Retrieved from https://nextcity.org/features/view/is-unschooling-the-way-to-decolonize-education?fbclid=IwAR-1J8oggHbzxUTDTYmOjS_7Fa44Nq1roew0UE9mjo06EVw4gXkcAk-wCkVo

31 Macias, A. (2014, May 28). 15 pieces of advice from Maya Angelou. Business Insider. Retrieved from https://www.businessinsider.com/maya-angelou-quotes-2014-5

32 Kennedy-Moore, E. (n.d.) Kid confidence: Help your child make friends, build resilience, and develop real self-esteem. Retrieved from https://eileenkennedymoore.com/books-videos/kid-confidence/?fbclid=IwAR-3lXrQhYd_enPTMmvWQvf1u5lHl_Xn47vB-JzsKIDhl6D0tBN-j4H4n-YVM

33 Medina, J., Benner, K., & Taylor, K. (2019, March 12). Actresses, business leaders and other wealthy parents charged in U.S. college entry fraud. New York Times. Retrieved from https://www.nytimes.com/2019/03/12/us/college-admissions-cheating-scandal.html

34 Dalai Lama XIV quote. (n.d.). Retrieved from https://www.goodreads.com/quotes/26912-judge-your-success-by-what-you-had-to-give-up

35 Bell, J. (March 1995). Understanding adultism: A major obstacle to developing positive youth-adult relationships. (PDF). YouthBuild USA Retrieved from https://actioncivics.scoe.net/pdf/Understanding_Adultism.pdf

36 DiAngelo, R. (2018). White fragility: Why it's so hard for white people to talk about racism. Retrieved from http://www.beacon.org/White-Fragility-P1346.aspx

37 https://www.alfiekohn.org/article/five-reasons-stop-saying-good-job/; For more reading and research about the problems with praise, read Alfie Kohn's Punished by Rewards: The Trouble with Gold Stars, Incentive Plans, A's, Praise, and Other Bribes (Boston: Houghton Mifflin, 1993 / 1999 / 2018)

38 Dweck, C.S. (2008). Mindset: The new psychology of success [Google Books version]. Retrieved from https://books.google.com/

39 McCready, A. (n.d.). Encouraging words. Retrieved from https://www.positiveparentingsolutions.com/parenting/encouraging-words

40 Kohn, A. (2012, February 3). Criticizing (common criticisms of) praise [Blog post]. Retrieved from https://www.alfiekohn.org/blogs/criticizing-common-criticisms-praise/

41 Kohn, A. (2006). Unconditional parenting: Moving from rewards and punishment to love and reason [Kindle version]. Retrieved from http://www.amazon.com/

42 https://www.5lovelanguages.com/

43 https://www.heysigmund.com/developmental-stage/

44 https://stylecaster.com/bts-masculinity-america/

45 https://www.smithsonianmag.com/arts-culture/when-did-girls-start-wearing-pink-1370097/

46 https://artsandculture.google.com/exhibit/BQJSZR_j5AhtLA

47 Siegel, D. J. (2012). The whole-brain child: 12 revolutionary strategies to nurture your child's developing mind. Bantam.

48 https://www.newyorker.com/science/maria-konnikova/power-touch

49 Resting Bitch Face

50 Cohen, L. J. (2001). Playful parenting: A bold new way to nurture close connections, solve behavior problems, and encourage children's confidence. Ballantine Books. (p.6)

51 https://cindywangbrandt.com/podcast/episode-74-high-lights-of-the-parenting-forward-conference/

52 Cooper, M. (2015, December 1). The false promise of meritocracy. The Atlantic. Retrieved from https://www.theatlantic.com/business/archive/2015/12/meritocracy/418074/

53 Anderson, M.D. (2017, July 27). Why the myth of meritocracy hurts kids of color. The Atlantic. Retrieved from https://www.theatlantic.com/education/archive/2017/07/internalizing-the-myth-of-meritoc-racy/535035/

54 Blackburn, S. (2019, March 21). What is the model minority myth? Teaching Tolerance. Retrieved from https://www.tolerance.org/maga-zine/what-is-the-model-minority-myth

55 Veruca Salt is a character in Roald Dahl's Charlie in the Chocolate Factory, depicted as demanding and over-indulged by her rich, permissive parents.

56 Fluger. J. (2013, January 10). China's one-child policy: Curse of the 'little emperors.' Time. Retrieved from http://healthland.time.com/2013/01/10/little-emperors/

57 Beam, C. (2015, September 30). Children of the Yuan percent: Every-one hates China's rich kids. Bloomberg Businessweek. Retrieved from https://www.bloomberg.com/news/features/2015-10-01/children-of-the-yuan-percent-everyone-hates-china-s-rich-kids

58 Dudley Dursley. Harry Potter Wiki. Retrieved from https://harrypotter.
    fandom.com/wiki/Dudley_Dursley

59 Kohn, A. (2014). The myth of the spoiled child: Challenging the conven-
    tional wisdom about children and parenting. Da Capo Press

60 https://www.goodreads.com/quotes/6513242-nothing-is-more-despica-
    ble-than-respect-based-on-fear

61 Faure, G. & Fang, T. (2008). Changing Chinese values: Keeping up with
    paradoxes. International Business Review. 17, 194-207. DOI: 10.1016/j.
    ibusrev.2008.02.011.

62 https://dictionary.apa.org/unconditional-positive-regard

63 https://sites.google.com/site/paroaci/buddhism

64 Love, S. (2017, October 2). Science and Chinese somatization. Undark:
    Truth, Beauty, Science. Retrieved from https://undark.org/article/sci-
    ence-chinese-somatization/

65 Van der Kolk, B. A. (2014). The body keeps the score: Brain, mind, and
    body in the healing of trauma. Viking Press.

66 Tung, W.-C., & Li, Z. (2015). Pain beliefs and behaviors among Chinese.
    Home Health Care Management & Practice, 27(2), 95–97. https://doi.
    org/10.1177/1084822314547962

67 21 Surprising tiger facts prove these big cats are amazing. (n.d.) In Ani-
    mal Planet. Retrieved from http://www.animalplanet.com/wild-animals/
    tigerpedia/tiger-facts-prove-big-cats-amazing/

68 Cook, G. (2013, October 22). Why we are wired to connect. Retrieved from
    https://www.scientificamerican.com/article/why-we-are-wired-to-connect/

69 https://qz.com/1570179/how-to-make-friends-build-a-communi-
    ty-and-create-the-life-you-want/?fbclid=IwAR0rEBlc39KVfbi8RcsOm-
    KezR1MYWnXjxws3q5vdd_PceV15NW6HZf_Ugzc

70 Pearson, E. and Podeschi, R. (1997). Humanism and individualism:
    Maslow and his critics. Adult Education Research Conference. https://
    newprairiepress.org/aerc/1997/papers/35

71 https://lincolnmichel.wordpress.com/2014/04/19/maslows-hierar-
    chy-connected-to-blackfoot-beliefs/?fbclid=IwAR0wt9sY2Mj6FdfEIB-
    NoYzlHIBT5sas70mk3piYT9M8MvaLjJAREc-ofmTg

72 https://lincolnmichel.files.wordpress.com/2014/04/slide19.jpg

73 Ford, B. et al (2015). Culture shapes whether the pursuit of happiness
    predicts higher or lower well-being. Journal of Experimental Psychology:
    General, 144(6), 1053–1062. https://doi.org/10.1037/xge0000108

74   Ford, B. et al (2015) p. 1054

75   Venniro, M. et al. (2018). Volitional social interaction prevents drug addiction in rat models. Nature Neuroscience, 21(Nov), 1520–1529. https://doi.org/10.1038/s41593-018-0246-6

76   Teo, A. R., Choi, H., & Valenstein, M. (2013). Social relationships and depression: Ten-year follow-up from a nationally representative study. PLOS ONE, 10. https://doi.org/10.1371/journal.pone.0062396

77   Umberson, D., & Karas Montez, J. (2010). Social relationships and health: A flashpoint for health policy. Journal of Health and Social Behavior, 51(1_suppl), S54–S66. https://doi.org/10.1177/0022146510383501

78   https://www.socialconnectedness.org/social-science-101-this-is-your-brain-on-social/
https://www.livescience.com/58935-social-neuropeptides-oxytocin-dopamine-endorphins.html

79   NIDA. (2018, October 15). Study shows impact of social interactions on addictive behavior. Retrieved from https://www.drugabuse.gov/news-events/news-releases/2018/10/study-shows-impact-of-social-interactions-on-addictive-behavior

80   Rojas, M. (2018). Happiness in Latin American has social foundations. In Sachs, J.D., Layard, R. & Helliwell, J.F. (Eds.) World Happiness Report (pp 114-145). Working Papers id:12761, eSocialSciences. https://s3.amazonaws.com/happiness-report/2018/CH6-WHR-lr.pdf

81   https://ourworldindata.org/mental-health#depression

82   https://www.ncbi.nlm.nih.gov/pmc/articles/PMC3839668/
Steele, L., & Lynch, S. (2013). The pursuit of happiness in China: Individualism, collectivism, and subjective well-being during China's economic and social transformation. Social Indicators Research, 114(2), 441-451. Retrieved from http://www.jstor.org/stable/24720256

83   Barton. D.W. (2017, March 29). Concept of uchi-soto: In-groups and out-groups. Japanology. Retrieved from http://japanology.org/2017/03/concept-of-uchi-soto-in-groups-and-out-groups/

84   Fisher, M. (2013, October 24). China's bystander problem: Another death after crowd ignores woman in peril. Washington Post. Retrieved from https://www.washingtonpost.com/news/worldviews/wp/2013/10/24/chinas-bystander-problem-another-death-after-crowd-ignores-woman-in-peril/?noredirect=on

85 https://people.howstuffworks.com/culture-traditions/national-traditions/chinese-tradition4.htm

86 https://www.deseretnews.com/article/563689/Junk-values-are-trashing-families-psychologist-says.html

87 https://www.instagram.com/jameelajamilofficial/?hl=en

88 https://www.parent.com/330509-2/

89 https://www.newworldencyclopedia.org/entry/Gift_economy

90 https://buynothingproject.org/about/mission-and-principles/

91 https://www.facebook.com/groups/UntigeringParents

92 https://www.statista.com/statistics/254857/child-abuse-rate-in-the-us-by-race-ethnicity/

93 Coates, T. (2015). *Between the world and me.* Spiegel & Grau.

94 Alexie, S., & Forney, E. (2007). *The absolutely true diary of a part-time Indian.* Little, Brown.

95 Seo, D. (1995, December 27). Growing Asian enrollment redefines UC campuses : Education: Their influence has increased with visibility. But affirmative action rollback fuels backlash fear. *LA Times. Retrieved from* https://www.latimes.com

96 Whitman, W. (1892). *Song of Myself.* Retrieved on 28 August 2019 from https://www.poetryfoundation.org/poems/45477/song-of-myself-1892-version

97 https://www.yellowstonepark.com/things-to-do/wolf-reintroduction-changes-ecosystem

For more untigering thoughts,
subscribe to Iris' blog at
www.untigering.com